USING EDUCATIONAL CRITICISM AND CONNOISSEURSHIP FOR QUALITATIVE RESEARCH

Using Educational Criticism and Connoisseurship for Qualitative Research develops the practical elements of educational criticism, a form of qualitative inquiry that takes its lead from the work that critics have done in fields such as the visual arts, music, literature, drama, and dance. Written by leading scholars in the field of curriculum studies, and research methods, this book explores the interpretive and evaluative aspects of educational criticism, through which the educational critic offers means for understanding and attributing significance to educational events. Featuring chapter-by-chapter activities, guiding questions, and key terms, this volume addresses matters of study design, pedagogy, and trends in doing educational criticism and connoisseurship. By offering a uniquely in-depth account of this research method, *Using Educational Criticism and Connoisseurship for Qualitative Research* will be accessible to researchers and students in curriculum and instruction, educational leadership, and higher education.

P. Bruce Uhrmacher is Professor of Research Methods and Education at the Morgridge College of Education, University of Denver, USA, and Faculty Advisor for the Institute for Creative Teaching. He previously served as President of the American Association for Teaching and Curriculum. His research interests include arts-based research, qualitative research, alternative school settings, curriculum theory and practice, and Waldorf education.

Christy McConnell Moroye is Associate Professor of Educational Foundations and Curriculum Studies in the College of Education and Behavioral Sciences at the University of Northern Colorado, USA. She is Co-Editor of *Curriculum and Teaching Dialogue* and is interested in ecological and aesthetic perspectives of education.

David J. Flinders is Professor of Curriculum Studies at Indiana University, Bloomington, USA. His interests focus on qualitative research methods, secondary school reform, curriculum theory, and peace studies.

USING EDUCATIONAL CRITICISM AND CONNOISSEURSHIP FOR QUALITATIVE RESEARCH

P. Bruce Uhrmacher, Christy McConnell Moroye, and David J. Flinders

Routledge
Taylor & Francis Group

NEW YORK AND LONDON

First published 2017
by Routledge
711 Third Avenue, New York, NY 10017

and by Routledge
2 Park Square, Milton Park, Abingdon, Oxon OX14 4RN

Routledge is an imprint of the Taylor & Francis Group, an informa business

© 2017 Taylor & Francis

The right of P. Bruce Uhrmacher, Christy McConnell Moroye, and David J. Flinders to be identified as authors of this work has been asserted by them in accordance with sections 77 and 78 of the Copyright, Designs and Patents Act 1988.

British Library Cataloguing in Publication Data
A catalogue record for this book is available from the British Library

Library of Congress Cataloging in Publication Data
Names: Uhrmacher, P. Bruce., author. | Moroye, Christy McConnell, author. | Flinders, David J., 1955- author.
Title: Using educational criticism and connoisseurship for qualitative research / P. Bruce Uhrmacher, Christy McConnell Moroye, David J. Flinders.
Description: New York, NY : Routledge, 2016. | Includes bibliographical references.
Identifiers: LCCN 2016021491 | ISBN 9781138677630 (hardback) | ISBN 9781138677647 (pbk.) | ISBN 9781315559421 (ebook)
Subjects: LCSH: Education--Research--Methodology. | Qualitative research. | Critical pedagogy.
Classification: LCC LB1028 .U38 2016 | DDC 370.72--dc23
LC record available at https://lccn.loc.gov/2016021491

ISBN: 978-1-138-67763-0 (hbk)
ISBN: 978-1-138-67764-7 (pbk)
ISBN: 978-1-315-55942-1 (ebk)

Typeset in Bembo
by Taylor & Francis Books

To Elliot Eisner, mentor and friend

To my mother, daughter and friend

CONTENTS

ILLUSTRATIONS

Figures

Tables

ACKNOWLEDGMENTS

There are a number of people whom we wish to acknowledge, and while we cannot mention everyone, we do want to give a special thanks to Elise Wright, who assisted us in editing every chapter. Christy would like to send a big shout out to Jackson and Eric for putting up with her while she hid in the study for 24 hours at a time to write this book. Likewise Bruce thanks his kids, Arianna and Paul, and of course his wife Lisa, all of whom (for reasons that no one can fathom at times) put up with his quirky schedule and writing habits. David would like to thank God that the book is finally finished.

1

INTRODUCTION

Guiding questions

- What is educational criticism and connoisseurship?
- What are the components of educational criticism?
- What are the functions of educational criticism and connoisseurship?

Introduction

The purpose of this book is to develop the practical elements of educational criticism, a form of qualitative inquiry that takes its lead from the work that critics have done in fields such as the visual arts, music, literature, drama, and dance. Largely conceptualized by Stanford professor Elliot Eisner (1933–2014),[1] the method is utilized worldwide. This approach is sometimes called *educational criticism and connoisseurship*. In the chapters that follow, we will make distinctions between criticism and connoisseurship; however, for the sake of convenience, we will usually use the shorthand terms *educational criticism* or simply *criticism* in referring to this particular species of qualitative research. We also note that at times we refer to the researcher as the critic and at other times as the researcher. We use the terms interchangeably.

Connoisseurship, criticism, and education

What is educational criticism and connoisseurship? Let's begin by taking a look at the word "connoisseurship." Connoisseurship is a private act in which to some degree we all engage. It entails the skills of using one's senses to apprehend a present experience and of making fine-grained distinctions. A novice watching baseball, for example, may not be able to tell what kind of pitch the pitcher throws across the plate. An experienced watcher of the game may note that the pitch is a fastball, a curveball, a slider, or something else. A veteran of the game may not only know what kind of ball was thrown but also how often this pitcher throws that type of pitch and how good the pitcher is at doing so. Whether we focus on sports, schools, classrooms, teaching styles, literary essays, or refrigerators, by paying attention we all become connoisseurs in those areas we care about. What also should be clear is that we are always on a continuum of experiential understanding. Someone may know more than we do, but as we develop our sensibilities, we soon find that we know more than many.

Connoisseurship, as we noted, is a private act, but generally, as human beings, we have a desire to share what we have learned. Here is where its counterpart criticism comes into play. Criticism is the disclosure of what we learned through our connoisseurship. The word "criticism" is derived from the Greek *krino* "to judge" and *krites*, "a judge or juryman" (Welleck 1981: 298). The idea of judging literature seems to have been utilized as early as the 4th century BC. Over time, criticism would take on new material to judge such as dance, theatre, and film. Today we realize that one can judge almost any aspect of life. The intentional pairing of criticism and education would take place under the direction of Elliot Eisner in the mid 1960s. At that time, a full exploration of what it means to do criticism is brought to the fore. But we would note that in the United States one can find a most significant coupling – and perhaps the first – of criticism with education in 1934 in the then newly formed journal *Social Frontier: A Journal of Educational Criticism and Reconstruction*. Edited by George Counts and including on its board such distinguished scholars as John Dewey, Charles Beard, and Sidney Hook, the journal kept its title until 1939 when it then changed its name to *Frontiers of Democracy*. While the usage of criticism in the earlier title is not clearly delineated, there are several clues to its inclusion. The purpose of the journal as outlined by William Heard Kilpatrick is to "become the expressive medium of those members of the teaching profession who believe that education has an important, even strategic, role to play in the reconstruction of American society" (1934: 2). Reconstruction, the interest in "considering the broad role of education in advancing the welfare and interests of the great masses of the people who do the work of society" (p. 5), was the aim of the journal. To do that, it seems the authors believe criticism to be their chosen method of writing, a kind of discourse that "makes no pretense to absolute objectivity and detachment" (p. 4).

Elliot Eisner was not a reconstructionist, but he, too, sought a research method more interested in its ability to improve schools and classrooms rather than having a strong fidelity to traditional methodological concerns. Similarly, he would eschew objectivity. From Eisner's perspective, criticism is the art of disclosing what one has learned through his or her connoisseurship. The means through which educational critics relate their educational experiences have generally consisted of four interrelated elements: description, interpretation, evaluation, and thematics. In description, the educational critic uses narrative, often figurative or literary in character, to display the essential and often subtle qualities of the situation experienced. Critics render a situation or event to help readers participate in exercising judgment of its educational value. Descriptions of events experienced "freezes" aspects of life so that we may contemplate their meaning. While much of this book focuses on literary descriptions, in particular, we must point out that the descriptive section of an educational criticism could take many forms. The description of a school or classroom could be rendered in visual (photographs, film), auditory (tape recording), or other forms of representation. Some of the work being conducted under the banner of arts-based research would fit under the descriptive aspect of an educational criticism.[2]

The interpretive aspect in educational criticism explores the meanings and consequences of educational events. Unlike the poet, the novelist, or some educational researchers who argue that the interpretation is in the rendering, the educational critic does not let description alone tell the story. The critic uses ideas, models, and theories from the arts, humanities, or social sciences to provide the reader with means for understanding what has been described. Moreover, there is no one "true" interpretation. Rather, each interpretation uses different kinds of evidence to secure a valid reason why conditions may be significant.

The evaluative aspect of an educational criticism assesses the educational significance of events described and interpreted. Finally, thematics in educational criticism is related to generalizing in social science research. Rather than making formal generalizations, however, educational critics provide the reader with an understanding of the major themes that run through the educational matters being studied. In turn, these themes provide the reader with ideas or guides for anticipating what may be found in other places. These theories provide guidance, not prediction.

Educational criticism and other qualitative methods

Like many other forms of research, and qualitative approaches in particular, educational criticism is a subset of empirical, interpretive inquiry. It overlaps with approaches such as ethnographic and case study research because educational criticism often involves fieldwork and seeks to contextualize data by attending to the particulars of what educational critics observe. Another point of similarity is that educational criticism depends on "thick description." Critics describe their settings so that one gets a feel for what it is like to be there. As Eisner pointed out, description serves an epistemological function; it helps one know the setting in intimate detail. Finally, criticism requires that researchers interpret their data. While all qualitative researchers usually interpret their findings, many focus on attaining an emic point of view or what we call "seeing with" – that of the insider. What do classroom events mean in the eyes of the particular teachers and students involved? What does a textbook chapter, a lesson on linear equations, or a poem by Robert Frost mean for those asked to teach or learn them firsthand?

Educational critics also try to attain and render an insider's point of view. But critics are not fearful of providing an "etic" viewpoint ("seeing about") – that of the outsider. As the old saying goes, the fish may be the last to discover water since it is so embedded in it. Thus, an outsider's perspective often helps those within a system see that to which they have become blinded. The words "emic" and "etic" are derived from usage in linguistics (see Pike, 1954) and the social sciences (Morris et al., 1999). While we do not take issue with critics using social science terms generally and the words "emic" and "etic" specifically, we prefer to focus on terms from the arts and humanities. Thus, beckoning to the perceptive qualities of educational criticism, we use the terms "seeing-with" and "seeing-about."

Another distinction between educational critics and other qualitative researchers is the former's interest in evaluation and action. One purpose of evaluation is to recommend improvements to the educational environment that you are studying. In this sense, educational criticism has an action component. To borrow and modify a famous phrase, the point of criticism is not simply to interpret an educational setting in various ways, but to change it. Thus, educational criticism has a structure that often includes a combination of description, interpretation, evaluation, and thematics.

Functions of educational criticism

Thus far, we have provided a brief overview of educational criticism. In short, it is a qualitative research method that takes its inspiration and ideas from the arts and humanities. It entails description, interpretation, evaluation, and thematics. Its overall aim is to seek improvement in the real world. But now we turn to the purposes of educational criticism. What are its strengths and utilities?

As John Dewey (1934) noted in his book, *Art as Experience*, "the function of criticism is the reeducation of perception"; its aims encompass the active and difficult process "of learning to see and hear" (p. 328). One can *listen* to music inattentively, but to *hear* music is often an achievement. It requires discernment, analysis, and practice. In the arts, both perception and comprehension are achievements that usually require the types of skills and knowledge that lead to connoisseurship. Yet, as Dewey argued, such achievements in learning to see and hear are not limited to what we typically refer to as "the arts." Rather, they can be found whenever people care deeply about – and respond deeply to – an experience. This includes, for example, those who are passionate about sports and make the effort to become knowledgeable in the sport that interests them. It includes cooks who invest time and enduring attention to the qualities of the food they prepare. One can be a critic and connoisseur of wine, of gardening, of automobiles, or of schools and of classrooms. In the last chapter of this book, we also point out that educational criticism may be thought of simply as criticism, and in that regard it can be utilized to examine any setting that has an intention behind it such as therapy sessions and businesses, among other venues.

Educational criticism may be used to help us break down stereotypes by demonstrating variations among like cases. In the social world it is not uncommon to find complex and even contradictory tendencies within an "N of 1." We are referring not only to one school or one classroom, but also to a single individual. Here the aim is to make the familiar strange by undermining what we assume to be the shared characteristics. The aim is to *make the familiar strange*. One way of doing so is by demonstrating the complexity of situations and events. Again, the meanings of social and educational experiences are multilayered and there is often more than meets the eye. Critics can also make the familiar strange by naming or calling attention to what we take for granted. As the poet William Wordsworth ([1807] 1974: 188) wrote, "the world is too much with us," and like poetry, criticism may prompt us to make explicit our everyday experiences and otherwise tacit forms of knowledge.

Criticism may also serve a pedagogical function by offering a glimpse into the lives of students, teachers, school administrators, and the like. The often vivid nature of criticism provides a behind-the-scenes perspective which others may not be able to experience firsthand. In this sense, criticism helps *make the strange familiar*.

Finally, still another use of educational criticism is that it allows us to interpret educational products and events from particular theoretical standpoints. What does a "constructivist" approach, for example, look like in actual math classrooms? What do lesson plans designed to promote meta-cognitive thinking in painting involve, and how are such plans implemented in an art classroom? The point in addressing such questions is to inform both our perceptions – the ability to see and hear – as well as our understandings of the a priori knowledge that we bring to our perceptions.

Identifying the uses of criticism is important because they imply the criteria by which criticism is evaluated. For example, above we refer to the pedagogical functions of criticism. These functions suggest that educational criticism is *educational* in at least two ways. First, the focus of educational criticism is usually on education – that is, valued learning in or outside of schools. But we would note that criticism generally, and the ideas in this book specifically, can be utilized by qualitative researchers outside the field of education. Thus, this approach is educational in that its aim is to "teach" whoever the intended audience of the criticism is. Does the criticism offer fresh ideas or ways of understanding? Does it bring into focus something significant but which goes unnoticed? Does it raise the levels of connoisseurship by which we observe, interpret, and evaluate the complexities of professional practices? Finally, does it inform what we do?

Overview of the chapters

In order to address these and other issues of doing educational criticism, we have divided our book into six chapters. Chapter 2 examines connoisseurship in great depth, offering several terms to aid the researcher in understanding its various aspects. We also discuss and refute the critique that connoisseurship is an elitist activity. Finally, we also help the critic understand that connoisseurship exists on a continuum and that even novice researchers know more than most and are therefore emerging connoisseurs.

In Chapter 3, we discuss matters of study design. Here researchers will learn about the ways in which critics depend on perceptivity and how such perceptivity influences many aspects of the study, such as number of participants and length of time in the sites. We also discuss conceptual frameworks, and in particular we focus on the ecology of schooling and the instructional arc. Finally, we also examine ways of thinking about ethics in conducting this kind of work.

Chapter 4 explores description and interpretation, two ways of disclosing what one has learned through connoisseurship. Description is often thought of as "an account of" while interpretation is "an account for" (see Eisner, 1991). We consider the ways in which such literary approaches and aesthetic features enhance a criticism rather than "mask" a "true" rendering of an event or situation. We also address the simple yet complex questions of how to find patterns and what those patterns mean.

Chapter 5 takes a look at evaluation and thematics, two major pedagogical elements of an educational criticism. Along the way, we explore how various curriculum terms are useful to the educational critic and we also consider curriculum ideologies as a way to aid in perceptivity. In addition, we suggest that critics annotate their field notes rather than code them. Also in this chapter we examine matters of subjectivity, validity, and generalization.

In Chapter 6, we examine trends and variations in doing educational criticism and connoisseurship. In this chapter we note that some educational critics combine survey data and other methods – both qualitative and quantitative – with criticism. We also re-examine what may be learned from the tradition of literary criticism; and we also suggest some new possibilities for criticism such as auto-criticism, action research criticism, and the postmodern critical essay.

A note about the organization of chapters. In each, we provide guiding questions to help the reader focus on some of the major themes explored in it. We also end each chapter with activities that the reader may wish to try out in order to deepen her understanding of this text. Finally, we also include a highlighted box in each of the following chapters so that students of the method may focus on some key notions that are likely to be relevant for writing proposals, master's theses, doctoral papers, and dissertations.

Reflection questions and activities

1. What is your initial reaction to the terms connoisseurship and criticism? What more do you want to know about each?

2. Create a chart that compares and contrasts educational criticism with other forms of qualitative research, such as case study, ethnography, narrative inquiry, and portraiture. Include categories of comparison such as researcher stance, purpose of the study, forms of representation, audience, data collection tools, and organizational structures. As you read each chapter, add to and revise your chart.

3. Using an online search engine, locate several dissertations that use educational criticism as its methodology. Begin a list of topics and research questions and refer to the studies for examples of the elements discussed in the remaining chapters.

In discussing any qualitative research method, it is prudent to show that you know some background of an idea or theory. The concepts of connoisseurship and criticism both have rich histories worth noting.

Notes

1 For those unfamiliar with the works of Elliot Eisner, see Uhrmacher and Matthews (2005).
2 Barone and Eisner (2011) are more likely to view educational criticism under the heading of arts-based research.

References

Barone, T. and Eisner, E.W. (2011). *Arts based research*. Thousand Oaks, CA: Sage.

Dewey, J. (1934). *Art as experience*. New York: Perigee Books.

Eisner, E. W. (1991). *The enlightened eye: Qualitative inquiry and the enhancement of educational practice*. New York: Macmillan.

Kilpatrick, W. H. (1934). Introduction. *The Social Frontier: A Journal of Educational Criticism and Reconstruction*. 1(1), 1–7.

Morris, M. W., Leung, K., Ames, D., and Lickel, B. (1999). Views from inside and outside: Integrating emic and etic insights about culture and justice judgment. *Academy of Management Review, 24*(4), 781–796.

Pike, K. L. (1954). Emic and etic standpoints for the description of behavior. In K. L. Pike (Ed.), *Language in relation to a unified theory of the structure of human behavior. Pt. 1 (Preliminary ed.)* (pp. 8–28). Glendale, CA: Summer Institute of Linguistics.

Uhrmacher, P. B. and J. Matthews (Eds.). (2005). *Intricate palette: Working the ideas of Elliot Eisner*. Columbus, OH: Merrill Prentice Hall.

Welleck, R. (1981). Literary criticism. In P. Hernadi (Ed.) *What is criticism?* (pp. 297–321). Bloomington: Indiana University Press.

Wordsworth, W. ([1807] 1974). The world is too much with us. In *The Norton anthology of English literature*. M. H. Abrams (Ed.). New York: Norton.

2

CONNOISSEURSHIP

The Arts of Perception and Discernment

Guiding questions

- What is educational connoisseurship?
- When and how does one become a connoisseur?
- Do I have to already be a connoisseur in order to conduct an educational criticism?
- What is the role of previous research and theory in educational criticism?

Introduction

This chapter focuses on connoisseurship, a concept that is central to educational criticism. The term connoisseur comes from the Latin word *cognoscere*, meaning "to know." A connoisseur is someone who knows about a particular domain. Such knowledge is foundational because it serves as both the means and ends of educational criticism. As we mentioned in the previous chapter, all educational research should be educational in at least two ways. Not only does it focus on education, but its purpose is to inform or to educate. It seeks to contribute to the growth of knowledge. We ask of research what it tells us about a particular phenomenon or event. Does it offer fresh perspectives or new ways of thinking? How does research advance or sophisticate our understandings of a given experience? Does it increase our discernment and appreciation of life in classrooms, teaching strategies, student motivation, school leadership, or the messages conveyed through curriculum materials and events?

In this chapter, our examination of connoisseurship is divided into three parts. First, we argue that the forms and functions of connoisseurship apply across a wide range of qualitative experience. Connoisseurship neither belongs to an exclusive group, nor is it limited to the arts, food, or fine wines. Second, we discuss the sources of connoisseurship. These sources include discernment, appreciation, and valuing. Discernment involves distinguishing qualities based on firsthand experience. In research, we often refer to these experiences as fieldwork. Appreciation includes knowledge of the conventions and cultural patterns that distinguish various genres of the context under study. Valuing points to the criteria used for understanding excellence with a given context. Finally, the chapter addresses uses of theory, calling attention to how theories may aid as well as hinder the development of connoisseurship.

What is connoisseurship?

Eisner (1991: 63) defines connoisseurship as "the ability to make fine-grained discriminations among complex and subtle qualities." This definition has two parts. First is the ability to discriminate. Wine connoisseurs are able to discriminate the qualities of a particular wine. Their senses, based in part on past experiences, are attuned to the taste of wine – its gustatory qualities – as well as the wine's color, nose, and surface tension (or "legs"). Their abilities guide their perceptions. Walter Pater ([1873] 1974), a nineteenth-century British essayist, emphasized the role of sensory experience in discriminating qualities by stating:

> In a sense it might even be said that our failure is to form habits: for, after all, habit is relative to a stereotyped world, and meantime it is only the roughness of the eye that makes any two persons, things, situations, seem alike. While all melts under our feet, we may well grasp at any exquisite passion, or any contribution to knowledge that seems by a lifted horizon to set the spirit free for a moment, or any stirring of the senses, strange dyes, strange colors, and curious odors, or work of the artist's hands, or the face of one's friend. Not to discriminate every moment some passionate attitude in those about us, and in the very brilliance of their gifts some tragic dividing of forces on their ways, is, on this short day of frost and sun, to sleep before evening.
>
> (p. 1620)

The second part of Eisner's definition concerns perceptions of "complex and subtle qualities" (1991: 63) as the subject or focus of connoisseurship. This part of the definition raises the question: What can one be a connoisseur of? We have already suggested that the uses of connoisseurship extend well beyond the arts, wine, and exotic cuisines. One can be a connoisseur on any subject or topic about which people care deeply and for which they develop an abiding interest. Candidates might include the arts, of course, but also cookbooks, digital technologies, mountain climbing, fashion, car hubcaps, architecture, coffee, or bonsai trees. Snow skiers, for example, care about the qualities of snow relevant to skiing. Avid basketball fans care about how a game is played, and not simply its final score; they are able to "read" strategies and configurations of play as they unfold on the court. Dog enthusiasts learn about breeds that interest them; they attend dog shows and talk with breeders.

Almost anyone, to some degree, is a connoisseur of something, but this is a matter of degree. At one end of the continuum are people who might take a fancy to a particular hobby or pastime, and who dabble in this interest on a surface level. At the other end are connoisseurs whose interests are consuming and enduring, perhaps across their lifespans. They may make these interests a professional concern to which they devote ongoing, conscientious, and systematic inquiry. In this sense, connoisseurship is not simply something that a person has or does not have. Rather, connoisseurship marks the quality of the relationship between the connoisseur and his or her area of expertise. We are not arguing that a connoisseur must hold advanced training or some type of certification. Sometimes formal training plays a significant role, but more important is that connoisseurs believe that their interests are worthwhile and shared by others who care about the quality of their engagement with these interests. It is on this basis that connoisseurs make efforts to increase their abilities to see and hear the full range of qualities that an experience affords. The process is one of learning to see and hear.

Learning to see and hear

The philosopher Gilbert Ryle (1956: 349) made a distinction between task verbs such as "to watch" and "to listen" and achievement verbs such as "to see" and "to hear." Task verbs refer largely to the mechanics of gathering sensory data. While watching and listening have both physiological and cultural dimensions, they often lack focused engagement and a guiding purpose. We may watch television out of boredom or listen to music as we clean the house. Achievement verbs imply a qualitatively different experience. We might observe Olympic performances, but fail to appreciate or "see" the high levels of skills that usually characterize Olympic achievements. We might listen to a jazz quartet without hearing the particular musical qualities that simultaneously characterize its genre and define the individual "signatures" of its performers. Attending a concert may guarantee the opportunity to listen to music, but sitting in the audience does not guarantee that the music will be "heard" and understood. The latter requires a more developed set of skills based on previous and direct experience. Such skills are a matter of combining perception with reason and affect to create what Jerome Bruner (1990) called "acts of meaning."

Achievement verbs represent abilities that depict what Eisner (1991) calls "epistemic seeing" (pp. 68–71). Drawing on Dretske (1969) and Polanyi (1967), Eisner argues that epistemic seeing is distinguished by an interdependence between sensory experience and ways of knowing. We should note that Eisner and Ryle use the terms "seeing and hearing" as shorthand for all of the senses, often in combination. Epistemic seeing grounds these sensory abilities in direct experience and, by doing so, broadens our conceptions of knowledge itself. Knowing often comes in the form of analytic and abstract propositions, such as in a physicist's search for the laws of nature. But knowledge is also embodied. It resides in actions as well as in thoughts – the act of drinking wine, attending a performance, direct study, or observing in schools.

Epistemic seeing points to the importance of observations and fieldwork to criticism as a form of research. Academic disciplines such as anthropology and archeology have long made fieldwork a rite of passage into these professions. The experience of "being there," with boots on the ground, so to speak, provides ways of learning about other cultures that cannot be gained through other means. In education, Peter Hlebowitsh (2012) argues this point in relation to how we evaluate classroom teaching. He suggests that today's trend of assessing teachers based on the standardized achievement scores of their students misses the point because it prevents under-standings of teaching "in relation to the particularities and subjectivities of a site and the collection of human beings that inhabit that site" (p. 2). In part, Hlebowitsh is arguing for a shift in the focus of assessment from outcomes to process. He also argues that this shift in focus calls for evaluators to reject the assumption that we possess any single, universal definition of good teaching because understanding what teachers and students do also entails how and why they do it. Context matters.

We will say more about the values that constitute excellence in teaching in a later section, but first want to expand the notion of "being there" as a way of knowing. On the one hand, most of us would be suspicious of a wine connoisseur who does not drink wine. We might wonder what the point of being such a connoisseur is to begin with. On the other hand, if one became a wine connoisseur simply by drinking a lot of wine, we would have many more wine connoisseurs than we do. Just as fieldwork is more than logging time with one's participants, learning from direct experience is also aided by tuition in the form of guidance from knowledgeable others.

If a person wants to learn about a type of painting, say mid-century abstract painting, it is a good idea to visit museums that have relevant collections. Better yet would be to visit these collections together with someone who is able to point out, bring to your attention, and explain the "visual language" that characterizes that genre. The aim of helping others learn is one of the reasons that museums employ docents. Learning to can food, to take another example, is likely to be learned in the kitchen by canning food. Yet, especially for the novice, an experienced relative or friend is likely to be close at hand to guide the novice and demonstrate the skills involved.

Sources of connoisseurship in education

Above we have argued three points. This first is that connoisseurship is grounded in the connoisseur's interests and belief in the importance of what he or she seeks to understand. Second, this understanding is built on firsthand, sensory experience. And, third, this direct experience can be enhanced by learning from the knowledge and skills of others. This last point is another way of saying that experience includes social and cultural dimensions. Its meanings depend, at least in a large measure, on the ways in which the experience participates in a cultural system. These systems lend experience its denotations and connotations, symbolism, values, and affective valiance. Tanney (2005) uses the example of coins and currencies to illustrate this point. While a child's first exposure to money is as an object, its significance rest in money's symbolic value and uses within an economic system. Once the child has grasped this significance, his or her understanding of money takes on new meanings and new uses. Three means of developing such cultural understandings are discussed below. They include discernment, appreciation, and valuing.

Discernment

This is the ability to notice and differentiate qualities. It is commonplace to how people interact with the historical, cultural, political, social, and economic milieu of which they are a part. We learn to discern the flavors, textures, and aromas of various foods; the auditory qualities of a person's voice; and the visual features of one's neighborhood or town. We learn to recognize the features of a friend's face, but not simply to be able to pick that person out of a crowd. Faces tell us much more. They provide nonverbal clues that we learn to "read" or interpret for information about how a person is feeling, their attitudes, and that person's relationships with others. Such discernment may be largely unconscious, which we will say more about shortly. We will say more about implicit knowledge as well. Here, our point is that while reading facial expressions involve the physiology of our sensory apparatus, it is a learned ability and as such relies on the conventions of shared meaning.

For example, we feed infants foods that we believe are appropriate and nutritious for that age. Biology may account for what makes the food nutritious (proteins, calories, etc.), but appropriateness means more than the food is digestible and that it contributes to physical growth. We seek food that we believe the infant will enjoy – food that tastes good – and this belief often closely aligns with foods that are commonly fed to infants and which we ourselves were fed at that age. Here appropriateness is a function of custom as well as science. Under the right conditions, infants can learn to eat and enjoy (even crave) caviar or puréed oysters. Such foods may be nutritious and available (for some), but they do not fit our conventional categories of "baby food."

Classroom lessons and formal educational settings are also shaped by culture and custom. Because education is social, it reflects cultural norms, values, rituals, traditions, local histories, politics, and identities. Such factors are what make schooling so complex and potentially rich in meaning. At the same time, the sociocultural side of experience is neither static nor uniform. Rather, it changes over time in ways that make no two lessons, teachers, or students exactly alike. In one classroom, the teacher may signal the beginning of class by her posture and position at the front of the classroom. Other teachers may begin lessons in other ways – a standard greeting or with a ritual of handing back assignments. Culture is shared, but expressed in ways that allow teachers to put their own imprint on their work; students interpret curriculum materials in nuanced ways; and intricate histories emerge as lessons, days, and weeks unfold.

Again, recognizing such nuanced meanings is an achievement that does not follow from simply being exposed to a given set of qualities. One important reason for this is that much of our day-to-day lives depend on knowledge that involves little or no conscious thought. Discernment is thereby lost to routines and repetitive actions. Driving a familiar route home or brushing one's teeth are such habitual activities that they can often be accomplished without much conscious attention at all. Their tacit nature holds a great deal of practical advantage by freeing our attention and allowing us to focus conscious thought on other matters.

Educational experience, in the sense of active learning, is different. Routines pervade schooling, but they may or may not be educational. For John Dewey (1938), educational experiences must possess two qualities. First, they are marked by meaningful engagement. They denote experiences in which groups and individuals intently take part in solving problems, formulating questions, identifying resources, acting, and then reflecting on that action. Dewey's second criterion for an educational experience is that it led to some form of moral, social, or academic growth. That is, education changes people. It allows them to act more intelligently and compassionately in the future. Experiences undergone in the present are carried forward in the form of such skills and abilities.

Dewey (1938) further argued that:

> Perhaps the greatest of all pedagogical fallacies is that a student learns only the thing he or she is studying at a particular time. Collateral learning, in the way of likes and dislikes may be and often is much more important than the spelling lesson or lesson in geography or history that is learned. For these attitudes are fundamentally what count in the future.
>
> *(p. 48)*

What Dewey refers to as collateral learning today is called the implicit or "hidden" curriculum. Rather than a matter of explicit or didactic instruction, the implicit curriculum is learned from the overall situations in which they are embedded. To put this another way, implicit lessons are often learned from the way schools are. The classroom environment, its social organization, the distribution of power and status, modeling, and relationships all convey tacit meanings about what is going on in classroom settings. Frequently these messages signal the particular types or genres of well-established patterns of interacting that we can label as lectures, small-group activities, demonstrations, whole-group discussion, and so forth. Although such patterns become so familiar that we rarely need to label them as they occur, they quietly take their place among the defining features of school experience.

The most common instance of labeling or naming such frames (this is a lecture; this is a demonstration) is when these assumptions break down. In this sense, the implicit curriculum is like the glass pane of a window. As long as the window is "working," we look *through* it, not *at* it. If it becomes covered or broken, then we notice. Its lack of transparency becomes an explicit problem to be solved, as when cultural differences prompt us to question otherwise unspoken assumptions. Yet when the window is working, its pane may not exist in conscious thought as our attention is drawn to whatever lies beyond its frame. What is habitual and taken for granted comes to elicit automatic responses for the very reason that it is so common. As William Wordsworth (1888) put this: "The world is too much with us; late and soon, Getting and spending, we lay waste our powers."

Appreciation

This is a matter of knowing what to look for. In common usage, we might say to a friend, "I appreciate your situation," in order to express our understanding and consideration. In doing so, we imply two types of knowledge. The first type seeks to recognize the particulars of the case at hand. In this instance, to appreciate another person's situation is to locate it within the immediate context of specific events, people, and places. We use this context to make sense of or identify reasons for the behavior of others as well as our own reasons for actions. Appreciation also involves a second type of contextualization, for every individual case is a case of something. It both stands on its own merits and participates, as we have argued, in the categories and traditions of which it is a part.

Most forms of qualitative experience participate in such traditions. In the arts, for example, Shakespeare's *Macbeth* is more than simply a dramatic narrative; it is the type of narrative that we call a tragedy. The traditions of the genre date back at least to Aristotle's analysis of tragedy in the *Poetics*. Such traditions offer a common language, set of expectations, and family of related concepts, in this case, concepts such as human fallibility, hubris, revenge, and catharsis. Connoisseurs of a style of painting use other concepts in their analysis of a particular work, including line, color, form, balance, and perspective, for example. These analytic tools position an individual painting or drama within an array of other works that help define its respective genre. In this respect, appreciation is discernment informed by such traditions.

Instructional methods and classroom lessons usually follow patterns characteristic of lesson types – class discussions, demonstrations, Socratic dialogue, and so forth. Socratic dialogue and demonstrations both use questioning strategies, but they do so in different ways and to achieve different ends. Classroom recitations use questions in still another way, and researchers (e.g. Shuy, 1986) have identified sub-patterns within this genre. Given such differences, it would be a mistake to judge a small-group discussion using criteria suited to lectures, and vice versa. This differentiating of criteria allows for more sophisticated and informed understandings than would otherwise be possible.

Appreciation, as we are using the term here, is a matter of knowing "how the game is played." It may involve understanding how different strategies can be used to achieve similar ends, the role of specific skills, or the ability to assess a player's particular strengths. We are using the terms "game" and "player" as metaphors for various types of social actions. But staying with a sports analogy, it is worth noting that fans learn a specialized vocabulary – offence, defence, backfield, pass protection, T-formation, and so on – and use this vocabulary to discuss aspects of play. To name the game and label its recurrent patterns is to call attention to these patterns and alert our perceptions. Such specialized vocabularies are useful because they both describe and inform.

To cite another example, prior to the 1960s academic writers usually took the gendered nature of language for granted. Like the window pane, it was unseen. But the introduction and use of terms such as "sexist language" brought into focus ways in which words and phrases assume a masculine perspective. Today such language is still with us, but writers now strive to avoid gendered pronouns and similar terms. In addition, many academic journals have adopted policies to this effect. What once went unrecognized has become, for many, a matter of conscious reflection.

Valuing

This is a third source of connoisseurship. It represents a connoisseur's knowledge of what constitutes goodness within a particular domain of study. Educational connoisseurs proceed on the basis of two broad questions: What is going on here? And why is it important? The second question places its emphasis on valuing. Regrettably, the term criticism is often associated with fault-finding and negative judgments. However, this meaning of criticism is not inherent in the approach we are advocating. If anything, art critics often seek out exemplary works in order to illustrate artistic achievements.

Writing on the functions of art criticism, Dewey (1934) argues that:

> The function of criticism is the reeducation of perception of works of art; it is an auxiliary in the process, a difficult process, of learning to see and hear. The conception that its business is to appraise, to judge in the legal and moral sense, arrests the perception of those who are influenced by the criticism that assumes this task.
>
> *(p. 324)*

Dewey goes on to write:

> The moral function of art itself is to remove prejudice, do away with the scales that keep the eye from seeing, tear away the veils due to wont and custom, perfect the power to perceive. The critics office is to further this work, performed by the object of art.
>
> *(p. 325)*

A film critic does more than simply describe films. He or she may, for example, place a given film with the context of its production history, aims, and social messages. Such aspects of a film reflect the normative and political ecology of which it is a part.

Values play an important role in educational connoisseurship because education itself is unavoidably normative in both its means and ends. Its purpose is to help people become better adults, and it strives to do so in humane ways – ways that do not harm students or threaten their dignity. As critical theorists have pointed out (e.g. Apple, 2014; Valenzuela, 2005; Brantlinger, 2007), schooling can be mis-educational in the sense of limiting student opportunities, especially for low-income and marginalized groups. Yet this assessment too has a normative basis that depends on values such as equity and social justice.

People often disagree over what values should be given priority and how to decide that question (Noddings, 2003). Should schooling focus on personal growth or social needs? Should schools prepare students to fit into society, or to change society? Should the aims of schooling be to promote cognitive skills such as logical reasoning, and can this be achieved while simultaneously introducing the intellectual heritage represented in academic disciplines? Such questions rest on a range of completing values that supply educational connoisseurs with an array of different criteria for assessing educational materials and events.

Recognizing multiple rather than a single definition of educational excellence allows connoisseurs to adapt their criteria to the circumstances at hand. What do these teachers and students, for example, seek to accomplish in a given activity or lesson? What are their particular resources, and so on? Earlier we mentioned that it would be unfair to judge a small-group activity using the same criteria used to assess lectures or demonstrations. Knowing a range of values and the traditions of which they are a part helps connoisseurs hone in on issues of significance, thereby offering further insights into how teachers, students, and others make sense of their school experience. This advantage, however, is threatened if the connoisseur's own values harden into a single mold, becoming a personal bias that limits rather than aids perception.

The place of theory

At the outset we want to note that the word *theory* is used in multiple ways. In the social sciences, formal theories refer to concepts, distinctions, and propositions that stand in logical or axiomatic relation to one another. The aims of such theory are to explain, predict, and control. Festinger's (1957) theory of cognitive dissonance or Bandura's (1986) social cognitive theory are examples. At the other end of the spectrum are instances in which the term theory is used informally to describe a person's hunch or best guess. One might say to a friend, for example, "I have a theory about why Herb and Alice split up." Theories in this sense may even be tacit and unrecognized. Implicit theories operate in the background of both research and our everyday lives. As William James reportedly (Cook and Crang, 2007: 7) said, "You cannot pick up rocks in a field without a theory."

Whether formal or not, theories are conceptual tools that serve a number of functions. First, as we have already suggested, theories call attention to relationships and patterns that might otherwise be missed. Different theories of motivation, for example, not only call for attention to rewards and punishments (behavioral rein-forcements), but also to "locus of control" in the form of attributions of success and failure, or what Lepper and Greene (1978) called "the hidden costs of rewards." Second, theories allow us to structure and organize perceptions and experiences, typically in the form of narratives or metaphors. Even a simple metaphor such as "computer memory" provides an implicit schema that likens digital retrieval with the common experience of human memory. Or we make sense of a situation by forming a chronology of its antecedents. In research, we call these processes analysis and interpretation. Third, theory is a way for researchers to frame their work in ways that connect it with other research in the field. Finally, theories provide a sense of satisfaction and psychological unity by bringing order to otherwise disparate or confusing situations.

However, like values, theories present researchers and connoisseurs with a double-edged sword. As Eisner (1991: 67) put this, "Labels and theories are a way of seeing. But a way of seeing is also a way of not seeing." His point applies to all sorts of tools. Early humans with a fondness for fruit learned that they could use a stick to knock fruit from the higher branches of tall trees; their stick/tool extended their reach. Yet with this advantage we also lost the ability to feel the fruit to determine its ripeness. In research, the trade-offs of theory are that it focuses attention in order to open new avenues of inquiry. Thereby theory contributes to connoisseurship. For the same reason, theories can blind us to what they put out of focus or neglect. Here the relationship of theory to practice is like the relationship between the foreground and background of a visual field. We habitually place much of our day-to-day experience in the background of our awareness in order to selectively focus our attention on whatever is in the foreground at a particular time.

A metaphor from American history serves to illustrate this point. "Westward expansion" is a metaphor that describes the migration of nineteenth-century European settlers. Yet this metaphor also tacitly reproduces their point of view – a point of view derived from the experience of those on the eastern side of the frontier. The metaphor does so by backgrounding other perspectives. For those on the western side of the frontier, their homeland is not expanding, but contracting. In short, metaphors exclude as well as include.

While different theories represent different perspectives, no single perspective is neutral or fully inclusive. The danger is in losing track of or failing to recognize this limitation. Dewey (1934) wrote that, "Recognition is perception arrested before it has a chance to develop freely" (p. 52). He was noting the propensity to recognize individual cases by placing them within the type of category to which they belong. A person might examine a tree for instance, recognize it as a river birch, and then move on. Painters, on the other hand, often take a different approach to "under-standing" the tree that he or she seeks to visually represent. In this case, the question is not what kind or type of tree it is, but rather what are the qualities of this particular river birch that make it distinctive and particular.

The problem of aborted perception due to the very conceptual tools that allow us to make sense of the world led Howard Becker (1993) to describe theory as a "necessary evil." It is tempting to take this position, because the limitations of theory seem contained with our conceptions of theory itself. By definition, theory is abstract, general, and parsimonious. People, art, and wine are specific, complex, and ever changing. Psychologists have no single theory adequate to explain even a single individual person. Rather, they have many theories – psychoanalytic theories, behavioral theories, theories of cognitive development, theories of affect, and so on. Multiple theories offer multiple perspectives. While each theory alone is limited, the threat of being blinded by theory is most likely when *a* theory becomes *the* theory that a connoisseur-researcher holds as a conviction rather than as a tool of perception. As Abraham Maslow (1966) said, "if all you have is a hammer, everything begins to look like a nail" (p. 15).

A final, related point is that the relationship between theory and perception is a two-way street. Educational theories promise to inform our perceptions, but our perceptions of particular cases "in the field" may also inform theory. With a theory of classroom management based on teacher authority, for example, a researcher may observe classrooms but find management strategies based on other factors (e.g. student needs). This lack of fit may be extreme in this case, but it is an example where theory falls short and needs revision. On this count, the best definition of theory may be that it is what researchers prove wrong. This task is how we increase the power and sophistication of theory, and why doubt, surprise, and alternative theories are so cherished in research. Without them, theories harden and hamper our perceptions. To put this another way, connoisseurs strive to see and hear what they do not expect to find.

Conclusion

In this chapter we have examined the concept of connoisseurship in relation to discernment, appreciation, valuing, and theory. Discernment is the ability to discriminate subtle and nuanced qualities. Appreciation involves knowing the conventions and traditions that characterize particular genres or types of qualitative experience. Valuing is represented by the knowledge of what constitutes goodness within a particular domain. In education we have no single model of excellence. Instead, we have multiple, sometimes competing models. Theory too, albeit limited, provides an array of positions from which to understand particular dimensions of school experience.

We summarize our main points with the caveat that the various topics discussed in this chapter partially overlap. First, there is nothing elitist about connoisseurship as we are using that term. All of us develop some level of connoisseurship in areas for which we have an abiding interest. Second, connoisseurship is a form of embodied knowledge that relies on direct sensory experience (discernment) combined with that ability to situate cases within the categories and contexts in which they participate (appreciation). Third, such knowledge and abilities are learned achievements. They require active and sustained efforts to put oneself in the way of specific experiences and reflect on those experiences. Fourth, we argue that the tools of connoisseurship can both aid and hinder its development, and therefore must be used flexibly or adapted to the context and particular aims of the inquiry at hand.

Connoisseurs are not able to enter these systematic experiences empty-headed, but they are able and should enter them open-minded.

Ultimately, connoisseurship is a private act in the sense that one can be a connoisseur and not share his or her understandings with others. To share, and thus increase the value of connoisseurship, is to make public the insights gained through connoisseurship. This process of making the connoisseurs' knowledge public requires a different skill set. We now turn to these skills in the following chapters.

Reflective questions and activities

1. Practice the art of seeing. Select a household or other familiar object and take five minutes to observe it. Try using all of your senses, or, for a variation, focus on one of your senses. What are you able to learn as a result of a focused experience? How will this help you become a connoisseur?

2. Try this: watch a movie on TV or at a theater. But, before you go to watch something, read a film review. The more extensive the film review, the better. Then watch the film and notice to what degree the film review guided your thoughts about the movie. In what ways did the review help you appreciate the movie? Do you think the review deepened your thinking about the movie? Also, do you think the review hindered your experience of the movie? If so, in what ways?

> All of us are connoisseurs in areas in which we have an abiding interest. The sources for connoisseurship include discernment, appreciation, and valuing. There is nothing elitist about connoisseurship. Connoisseurship is embodied sensory experiences combined with a cognitive skill to situate cases within categories and contexts. Connoisseurship can both assist and hamper our understanding of a context or phenomenon and must be used flexibly.

References

Apple, M. W. (2014). *Official knowledge: Democratic education in a conservative age* (3rd ed.). New York: Routledge.

Bandura, A. (1986). *Social foundations of thought and action: A social cognitive theory*. Englewood Cliffs, NJ: Prentice Hall.

Becker, H. (1993). Theory, the necessary evil. In D. J. Flinders and G. E. Mills (Eds.), *Theory and concepts in qualitative research: Perspectives from the field* (pp. 218–229). New York: Teachers College Press.

Brantlinger, E. (2007). (Re)Turning to Marx to understand anger among "winners" in schooling: A critical social psychology perspective. In J. A. Van Galen and G. W. Noblit (Eds.), *Late to class: Social class and schooling in the new economy* (pp. 235–268). Albany, NY: State University of New York Press.

Bruner, J. S. (1990). *Acts of meaning*. Cambridge, MA: Harvard University Press.

Cook, I. and Crang, M. (2007). *Doing ethnographies*. Los Angeles, CA: Sage.

Dewey, J. (1934). *Art as experience*. New York: Perigee Books.

Dewey, J. (1938). *Experience in education*. New York: Touchstone.

Dretske, F. (1969). *Seeing and knowing*. London, UK: Routledge & Kegan Paul.

Eisner, E. W. (1991). *The enlightened eye: Qualitative inquiry and the enhancement of educational practice*. New York: Macmillan.

Festinger, L. (1957). *A theory of cognitive dissonance*. Redwood City, CA: Stanford University Press.

Hlebowitsh, P. (2012). Being there: The ontological measure of teaching. *Curriculum and Teaching Dialogue*, 14(2), 1–12.

Lepper, M. R. and Greene, D. (1978). *The hidden costs of reward: New perspectives on the psychology of human motivation*. Hillsdale, NJ: Erlbaum Associates.

Maslow, A. (1966). *The psychology of science*. Chicago, IL: H. Regnery.

Noddings, N. (2003). *Happiness and education*. Boston, MA: Harvard University Press.

Pater, W. ([1873] 1974). The Renaissance. In In M. H. Abrams (Ed.), *The Norton anthology of English literature* (pp. 1633–1646). New York: Norton.

Polanyi, M. (1967). *The tacit dimension*. London, UK: Routledge & Kegan Paul.

Ryle, G. (1956). Sensation. In H. D. Lewis (Ed.), *Contemporary British Philosophy* (3rd ed.) (pp. 349–362). London, UK: George Allen and Unwin.

Shuy, R. (1986). Secretary Bennett's teaching: An argument for responsive teaching. *Teaching and Teacher Education*, 2(4), 315–323.

Tanney, J. (2005). Gilbert Ryle. In E. N. Zalta (Ed.), *The Stanford Encyclopedia of Philosophy online*. Retrieved from http://plato.stanford.edu/archives/spr2015/entries/ryle (last accessed: February 15, 2016).

Valenzuela, A. (2005). Subtractive schooling, caring relations, and social capital in the schooling of U.S.–Mexican youth. In L. Weis and M. Fine (Eds.), *Beyond silenced voices: Class, race, and gender in the United States schools* (pp. 83–94). Albany, NY: State University of New York Press.

Wordsworth, W. (1888). This world is too much with us. In *The complete poetical works* (p. 188). London, UK: Macmillan.

3

STUDY DESIGN

Guiding questions

- What do educational critics do?
- How do they select participants and a research site?
- How do they plan and arrange for the types of fieldwork that will inform their study?

Introduction

In Chapters 1 and 2 we gave an overview of educational criticism, as well as a closer look at the meanings and aspects of connoisseurship. In this chapter, we turn toward study design to provide a description of what the critic actually does. We treat the research process as a rich experience in itself, worthy of careful attention. Therefore, we offer fresh ways of thinking about the research process, including selecting a topic, conceptualizing your design through various frameworks, crafting research questions, finding participants, collecting data, and gaining access.

As you begin to conceptualize your study, you will be asking yourself questions about method and procedure. Before we articulate specifically what an educational criticism often entails, we offer several of Eisner's (1998) premises upon which he built this methodology.

1   There are multiple ways in which the world can be known: Artists, writers, and dancers, as well as scientists, have important things to say and tell about the world.
2   Human knowledge is a constructed form of experience and therefore a reflection of mind as well as nature: Knowledge is made, not simply discovered.

3   The forms through which humans represent their conception of the world have a major influence on what they are able to say about it.

...

6   Educational inquiry will be more complete and informative as we increase the range of ways we describe, interpret, and evaluate the educational world.

(pp. 7–8)

The above premises help us think about the role of the researcher, his/her associated skills, and the purpose of inquiry. An educational critic serves a unique role in the landscape of educational research, alongside phenomenologists, ethnographers, and others. While the ethnographer may focus on cultural behaviors, and the phenomenologist may privilege the meaning of the lived experience, the educational critic focuses upon the perception of qualities, interpreting their significance, and appraising their value, all toward educational ends. In short, the educational critic helps others see and understand what may otherwise go unnoticed.

Selecting a topic

Educational connoisseurship and criticism has been used to explore a wide range of topics. From adventure education (Ingman, 2013) to implications of state testing (Conn, 2014) to instructional adaptation (Flinders, 1987), the educational critic has many options. And although some settings are naturally bursting with sensory opportunities, many mundane activities may be brought to life by the skilled researcher. Consider this example from Ingman's (2013) study of adventure education:

> Pedro swings his pack around his arm, allowing it to thump onto his back. He staggers off to the side three steps before stopping the momentum of the pack and regaining his balance, the enormous bag still hanging on one shoulder. A friend supports him by grabbing his side. He leans forward, and pushes the weight of his pack up, balancing it on top of his back as he pushes his arms through the unfamiliar straps. He stands up straight, and the momentum of the heavy pack carries him backward a step – his young frame no match for the massive weight of four days of food, clothing and shelter. He leans forward again to regain some semblance of a center of gravity, and fidgets with his trekking poles – looking at the straps and feeling the grips. "How's that pack feel Pedro?" I ask him. He smiles through his response, "Heavy."
>
> *(pp. 105–106)*

Recalling Chapter 2, the topic of study will be largely influenced by the researcher's connoisseurship. If one has spent extensive time in classrooms, that environment will be readily seen by the critic. Educational criticism lends itself particularly well to topics that provide novel ways of seeing "common" educational practices. For example, Moroye (2007) observed "traditional" high school teachers who were ecologically minded. Although the classroom practices were not necessarily innovative and new, seeing them through an ecological lens offered a different way of thinking about the teachers' work. Similarly, Conrad (2011) observed culturally responsive teachers to further bring to light how such practices are enacted and problematized.

Educational criticisms also lend themselves well to topics that help us make connections and create anticipation for what we might see in other educational situations. Just as Eisner asked, "What do the arts have to offer education?" an educational critic might ask, what might community centers contribute to classroom organizations? How do the features of a unique setting inform our thinking about other educational settings? Uhrmacher's (1991) study of Waldorf schools asked just this question. He not only wanted to uncover what happens in actual Waldorf schools, but also he wanted to draw implications for public K-12 schools.[1]

Conceptualizing your design

Our focus in design will be to prompt researchers toward studies that may resemble other qualitative approaches but with an eye toward alterations that make the educational criticism come to life. Further, in the spirit of pragmatism, the educational critic hones in on the experience of all involved: the researcher, the participants, the community, and future readers. Thus, the research itself is open to possibility and to embracing the "unknown unknowns" (Pryor, 2010: 169) with an eye toward the pedagogical purposes of the criticism itself.

Although educational criticisms may take many forms, we offer two frameworks that originate with Eisner's curriculum and evaluation work: the school ecology and what we call the *instructional arc*.

Eisner's school ecology

We provide a framework that may be used to guide observations and interviews, based upon the classroom ecology, which includes curriculum, pedagogy, school structure, evaluation, and intention (Eisner, 1998). Briefly, the curriculum refers to content; pedagogy is about how the content is mediated (large group, small group, lecture, etc.), and school structure refers to time and space. How long is the class? Are seats bolted to the floor? Evaluation may refer to formal and/or informal styles of evaluation, and intentions are about aims and goals. What is supposed to happen in the classroom?

One point about this framework is that each dimension interacts with the others. If a teacher changes the way he teaches (pedagogy), then all of the other dimensions are affected as well. Consider what happens when teachers move from a lecture format to an inquiry-oriented style of teaching. In this scenario the changes in pedagogy affect time and space. Students engaged in inquiry often need more time to explore materials, and the furniture in the room may become inadequate for such explorations. It is the interactive effects of the ecology that makes these dimensions fit together as a conceptual framework. That is, they are not a laundry list of things to focus upon in observations and interviews, but rather a way of understanding the dynamic interactions and relationships at work.

We might also note that while the framework is useful in and of itself, it is not set in stone. Some researchers may want to consider Eisner's ecology of schooling and adapt its framework to fit other settings, a point we return to in our last chapter. Denison (1994), for example, dropped evaluation and reframed school structure and focused on curriculum, pedagogy, and the forum (setting) structure. Uhrmacher (1991) added the category of aesthetics to Eisner's ecology in order to refer to the kinds and qualities of materials used in the classrooms as well as their physical arrangements. Since Waldorf schools place a premium on the usage of natural and high-quality materials, the aesthetic category proved to be particularly helpful. At another time, Uhrmacher and Matthews (2005) added school/classroom–community relationships to Eisner's ecology framework to account for the fact that the community often impacts what takes place inside the classroom. In this case, they noticed that one school district in Colorado undertook years of work producing materials for an outcomes-based education, only to have it overturned by a school board that had not been paying attention. Thus, when undergoing change, communication to the larger community needs to be clear and ongoing. In this case, by not paying attention to school–community relations, each of the other dimensions was affected.

Another category that could be added to Eisner's framework is "administration." Often administrative imperatives are a dominant force and some researchers may choose to understand how this happens. There is, then, nothing sacrosanct about Eisner's ecology. He noted that other dimensions of classroom life could be found, but he believed the ones he focused on were dominant and fairly encompassing. We agree, but we would add that when another set of concerns arise, researchers may choose to modify Eisner's ecology to fit their needs.

The instructional arc

In our own work, we have often utilized Eisner's ecology of schooling along with a separate but related framework. First, we borrow "intentions" from the ecology and focus on it as part of three aspects of curriculum: the intentional, the operational, and the received. In other words, what do teachers desire/plan to happen? What actually happens? What did the students learn/experience? We call this the instructional arc.

Educational critics may look at the entire arc, or they may choose to focus upon one or two aspects. This is an important point, especially since it is often the case that we are eager to know what students take away from an experience. We often resort to tests just for this purpose. But we argue that one needs to know the aims and goals of a school or of a teacher before jumping to the results of tests. Further, the received curriculum is far richer than what may be found in a test score. How

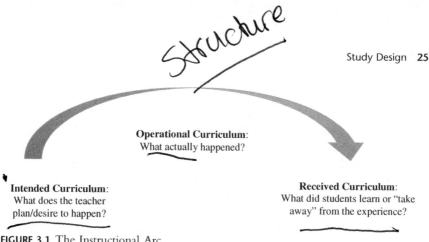

FIGURE 3.1 The Instructional Arc

did the students engage with the content and with each other? How do they describe what they learned and how? What do they want to do next? Moreover, the instructional arc provides us a way a seeing what actually happens in schools, with a focus on discerning congruence or variance between intentions and operations (see Thornton (1988) for an excellent example of this point).

Attending to all aspects of the arc may be too broad and time-intensive for certain studies. Many dissertations, for example, have been designed to look at just one or two aspects of the arc. Conrad (2011), for example, asked "What are the intentions of culturally responsive teachers?" and "How does culturally responsive teaching operationalize in the classroom?" He did not explore the received curriculum directly, but rather honed in on the ways in which a teacher's dispositions influenced their intentions for students, and how those intentions materialized in the classroom.

What makes this arc particularly fruitful for the educational critic is that the teachers' intentions are not always stated or obvious. They are, in some cases, even unknown, or not fully conscious, to the teachers. To see such intentions operationalized takes a skillful eye. But the framework offers a simple concept in which to couch complex and subtle qualities of classroom life.

Crafting research questions

Once a general topic has been selected the research questions serve as a framework for the study. Such questions have import not only for the researcher, but also for the participants, the dissertation committee, and the future audience for the study (Pryor, 2010). Therefore, the questions should reflect a sophisticated inquiry stated in understandable terms.

Crafting research questions for an educational criticism is a first step in the researcher's demonstration of his/her perceptive abilities. The questions must make space for exploring the "unknown unknowns" (Pryor, 2010: 169) while simultaneously providing direction and shape to the study. It is important to know what one is not studying, as much as it is important to know what one is studying.

We offer four ideas to assist us in framing research questions: (1) the dimensions of the school ecology, (2) the instructional arc, (3) prefigured, and (4) emergent foci.

In addition to using the frameworks to conceptualize your design, the *dimensions of the school ecology* may be directly addressed in your research questions. Such questions could focus on one or more of the elements (intentions, curriculum, pedagogy, evaluation, structure, school–community relationships) and, importantly, the interactions among them. Similarly, while also useful in conceptualizing your study, the instructional arc could appear explicitly in your questions and could explore various aspects of one or more of the intended, operationalized, or received curricula.

Prefigured questions aim at a particular target or locus of attention. Such questions focus the researcher's concentration on a particular phenomenon (e.g. the qualities of student interactions) or can be co-created with participants. For example, if a teacher is seeking feedback on her use of technology, the inquiry could be a collaborative effort with significance for all stakeholders. Having a prefigured focus does not mean that surprise will be ignored–quite the opposite. The researcher would attend to unanticipated interactions and qualities and provide interpretations. Eisner (1998) has suggested areas of prefigured focus to include content, forms of representation, incentives and motivational tactics, and engagement. Other foci have included evidence of social justice (Barone, 2014); equality (Gutiérrez, 2014); perceptions of an evaluation system (Crecinik, 1997); the beliefs of the teacher (Moroye, 2007; Conrad, 2011); and Reggio-inspired instruction (Ganus, 2010).

Research questions that are designed to elicit emergent themes are open ended and exploratory but still provide a guide for the researcher's imagination. What is significant in an emergent inquiry is largely dependent upon the context, theory, and values brought by the researcher. She may be interested in how the physical environment of the school informs personal interactions, but her questions are not directed at specific kinds or interactions or structures. The researcher's perception of what is significant, according to Eisner (1998), "is a cognitive achievement; indeed, it is what distinguishes the expert from the amateur. Experts know what to neglect" (Berliner, 1988: 189). To hone one's perception of what is significant, Eisner suggests using a two-column observation technique in which the left column is filled with observations and details and the right column contains the researcher's interpretations of them. The notes allow the researcher's ideas to coalesce around themes and significant qualities of the situation.

We suggest several considerations as you craft your research questions. First, consider what is already known, what can be known, and what you want to know about your topic. Who you are as a researcher should inform the questions themselves; an educational connoisseur has particular experiences that inform his/her perception. The inquiry at hand should be appropriate to the experiences of the researcher.

Second, if you are selecting a conceptual framework or theoretical lens in advance of the study, such as an ecological perspective, ensure the questions will be well informed by, as well as a challenge for, that lens. In other words, ensure space for disconfirming evidence.

Third, consider Eisner's dimensions of schooling as a way to hone in on particular aspects of your topic and/or site. It may be useful to select a portion of the ecology and to focus on relationships between those elements.

Fourth, consider various aspects of curriculum that could be explored. For example, several educational criticisms ask what the intentions are of a particular kind of teacher, and then they explore how such intentions are operationalized in the classroom and/or received by the students. Working with the intentional, operational, and received curricula provides an arc for exploration without unnecessary restraints on what one might discover. Other types of curricula are also ripe for educational criticism: the hidden (what is required for success in school but not taught); the null (what is not taught); the explicit and implicit; the complementary (the stated and/or unstated beliefs of the teacher); and the shadow (a focus on what is disdained with attendant activities of reflection and seeking balance).

The questions may also lend themselves to the process itself of educational criticism. As discussed in Chapters 1 and 2, the educational critic describes, interprets, evaluates, and generates themes. The research questions should be amenable to such processes.

Finding participants and accessing sites

Similar to other forms of qualitative research, educational criticism requires a level of trust and respect between the researcher and the participants. Because much of the focus of educational critics is to unearth and bring to light subtleties that may otherwise go unnoticed, that trust and respect is particularly important; such "discoveries" may be new and perhaps uncomfortable or, at least, not yet considered by the participants. We therefore begin our discussion of access and participants with an overview of ways to think about ethics in qualitative research.

While many texts on ethics in qualitative research are available and worthy reads, we focus our discussion on issues for educational critics. In particular, we explore various types of working relationships with participants, including utilitarian, deontological, caring, and ecological (Flinders, 1992).

Honing our ethical literacy helps us "foresee ethical problems and work through those problems that unavoidably turn up as research efforts unfold" (Flinders, 1992: 101). Certain ethical frameworks are better matched than others to the particular demands of qualitative fieldwork and reporting, but we don't suggest one best system. Rather, we urge researchers to consider the four frameworks in terms of the ongoing decision-making processes involved in qualitative inquiry.

The utilitarian framework roots ethical judgment in the idea of greatest good for the greatest number of people; it is the bedrock of quantitative research and carries with it a technical vocabulary. This framework can be helpful in thinking about informed consent and recruitment, avoidance of harm, and confidentiality in writing the report. However, informed consent suggests that participant and researcher can predict entirety of study, which is not always the case in qualitative research.

A deontological framework is one in which "moral conduct cannot be fully validated on the basis of consequences alone" unlike the utilitarian (Flinders, 1992: 104). The action must conform to ethical standards outside of the test of producing good results. It must be consistent with an ethic of duty. Therefore, rather than informed consent, the researcher should operate through the principles of reciprocity, which includes a range of negotiated obligations and recognized agreements. This framework suggests the replacement of avoidance of harm with avoidance of wrong – therefore other ethical considerations like honesty must be considered.

A third framework may be described as relational ethics, the significance of which was brought to light with feminist scholarship. This framework assumes we should not locate the ethical authority in rules but rather in attachment and regard for others. While relational ethics may lead to desired results of a deontological or utilitarian perspective, the behavior should be informed by a caring attitude toward others. Collaboration rather than reciprocity is necessary to honor the interdependent nature of the research. The researcher and participants are engaged in receptivity and involvement, and the researcher is open to negotiation throughout the process of the research. The experience of confirmation is a nonjudgmental stance but does not preclude the researcher from making an evaluation.

Fourth, and finally, the ecological framework describes interdependent, rhizomatic relationships (Deleuze and Guattari, 1987). It requires attention to cultural and social groups and sensitivity to taken-for-granted aspects of our professional and social lives and identities. The ecological framework asks that we not only prevent harm, but that we also recognize individuals as part of a larger whole.

Finding participants

Finding participants can be a challenge, or at times, a starting point. For example, if a study is born from a curiosity about the practices of a particular teacher or a particular kind of teacher, such as ecologically or aesthetically minded teachers, then likely the researcher has some knowledge of such individuals. If studying like-minded practitioners, the snowball method may prove to be not only convenient, but prudent.

A common question for qualitative researchers deals with the appropriate number of participants, as well as their relevant qualities and demographics. In an analysis of 38 educational criticisms, the average number of participants was 38 with a range of 2 to 240. Excluding the outlier of 240, the average was about 12. However, 19 of the studies had between 2 and 8 participants. The right number for each study may be determined by a number of factors, including access and availability of participants, the nature of the context (e.g. individual teachers or schools), and the goals of the inquiry. As with other qualitative research methods, a large population is not necessarily required in order to discern significant qualities of the situation. As a general rule, we recommend a participant group of four, but of course this could vary.

Many critics seek to include a diverse array of participants by considering culture, gender, class, grade level, educational background, and other factors. These demographics become an important part of the description of the participants in the write-up of your study.

Various practical matters must be considered in order for the study to be feasible. An educational criticism may require significant time spent in research sites, so other practical matters come into play, such as geography and the desirable times to observe the activity. It may also be necessary for the researcher to visit during unexpected times, such as to observe an extra-curricular activity, so staying open to such possibilities is important. In regard to this issue of time, we also note that the important factor is not how long a researcher is at a site, but rather how quickly she can use her perceptivity in picking up the important qualities that matter. Traditionally, anthropologists might be at a setting for a long period of time, but not necessarily so with educational critics. We also point out that often participants at a setting do not want to be observed by researchers for a long period of time. From this point of view, brevity is an asset.

As educational critics, we also suggest access as a process, not an event. It takes time to build relationships and to maintain them throughout the duration of the study. "Access" includes initial site permissions, but also includes ongoing invitations to see additional events or to work with different participants. Participant selection may be an ongoing process; one does not need to secure all participants at the beginning of the study, and in fact there may be some benefit to an ongoing process of identification.

When seeking access, remember that access works differently in each site. We encourage researchers to understand access as a form of data collection. What kinds of official channels were necessary to find and talk with potential participants? How did participants, or gatekeepers, respond to the topic of your study and research questions?

Data collection: being there

It is important to consider your research questions and participants' schedules as you design your plan for data collection. You will want to consider the interaction between your observations, interviews, and artifact collection, as each informs and is informed by the others. Not only does such comparison enhance trustworthiness of the study, it guides your discernment of the qualities, priorities, values, and practices you are noticing.

Many educational critics begin with an interview and then schedule a series of observations over a number of weeks. In an analysis of 38 educational criticisms,

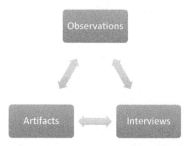

FIGURE 3.2 Relationships Between Data Sources

field observations ranged from two days to two months, with most falling between one to two weeks (several hours per day) per participant (classroom or other setting). However, this may vary depending upon the research questions, the participants' schedules, and the perceptive abilities of the researcher. In some cases, a shorter time frame has advantages, such as ease of gaining permission.

Fieldwork

Data collection tools help educational critics attend to significant qualities of the educational situation. Remembering that the role of the critic is to see and interpret subtleties, it is important for him/her to hone important perceptive abilities and to use appropriate tools that aid with that task.

Observations: being a sponge

What kinds of observations lead to a meaningful criticism? As a connoisseur, observations require a special kind of perception, one that attends to the events themselves as well as what the events do to our experiences. This perception is a kind of in-the-moment awareness, what Eisner calls "enlightened self-consciousness" (1998: 183).

To hone and activate such an awareness, we suggest several types of observational activities:

- the wide-angle lens;
- the multi-sensory experience;
- the single-sensory experience;
- the episodic vignette;
- lens-specific observation; and
- visual representations.

The wide-angle lens is a great place to begin. In this type of observation, everything is important. Start with a particular place – the northwest corner of a classroom or the tree on the south side of the activity field. Then work your way clockwise describing everything you see and hear. Your goal is to absorb and record the particulars of the setting. You are creating for yourself the context within which other observable events will happen.

As you engage in your wide-angle lens observation, you may want to try to achieve the multi-sensory experience. Describe each section of your environment using each sense. Much of your observation may need to be imagined or meta-phorically described. For example, you would not taste the walls of a classroom, but you could describe them as a sweet mint green, cold like an ice-cream cone. The descriptor elicits the senses of sight and taste without you violating any social norms. Be sure to consider the sources of your observations. Was the mint-green color choice that of the teacher? Does s/he like the color choice or try to cover it?

Is the color repeated throughout the room? If the wall had a sound what would it be? A splashing ocean? The cry of a young child?

A single sensory experience further deepens your perception of the environment. Select one sense you think has the potential to yield interesting ideas and try to observe using only that sense. You may choose touch, for example, and be interested in exploring the various textures of the room. You could observe the bubbled paint on the walls, the rough stretch of industrial carpeting, the smooth fabricated wood desk, the hot vent of the classroom computer. Some of these observations may need to be inferred and then checked at an appropriate time, or, again, an imaginative approach can yield interesting observations.

Once you feel well grounded in the observational spaces, you will be better equipped to notice the events and interactions of your participants. While recording the sequence of events as they unfold is a common and worthy practice, an educational criticism also thrives on vignettes. Occasionally writing such episodic vignettes in the moment may prove fruitful. This process involves selecting a starting point, which isn't always easy to identify. Perhaps it is a question asked by a student, an announcement made by the teacher, or an unplanned disruption that changes the course of events.

In your log, note the start of the vignette (a code such as VN is useful). Then describe the events in real time and present tense. Here's an example from Moroye's (2007) field notes:

VN START.

We then sit down in his comfy office with windows out to a courtyard for his first interview. Mr. Rye has energy energy energy.

During our interview a student walks in – it is as if she was Mr. Rye's long lost twin who had just returned from a trek across India. "Oh, so good to see you, Melanie! How ARE you?" he sings.

As time for class draws near, two more students come into his office, which is right across the hall from their class with Mr. Rye. One student yammers about a film he wants to make – Mr. Rye picks up every bit of energy and hangs on every word. A girl then walks in smiling to tell Mr. Rye she's going to the state university. She wants to know what dorm she should live in. Mr. Rye embraces her and engages the group in conversation until a bit after the bell rings. The three walk into class late together, still talking.

VN STOP.

Dialogue, facial expressions, body language, activity, and other details bring the vignette to life. Find a place to conclude the vignette – the resolution to a disruption, another question asked, the end of the activity – and label it as such in your log.

Each day of observations ends with work ahead! Go back while your notes are fresh and transcribe your observational notes to electronic text. Or, if you are typing your notes, edit, refine, annotate, and clean up your text.

If you are using a particular lens for your observations, such as one of social justice or ecology or cultural identity, then it may be fruitful to practice lens-focused observations, alongside general observations. For a set period of time, say 15 minutes, view your setting and participants with a strict theoretical lens. You would, for example, note all aspects of the setting that pertain to social justice issues and record such details. Then, immediately following that and for the same period of time, take more generalized observation notes. Be sure to code or annotate (see Chapter 5) these sections so that when you review your day's observations you may make comparisons between your observation periods. This juxtaposition will not only inform your findings, it will also help you see how the lens you are using informs what you choose to notice and record. You can problematize your assumptions by asking if you are really recording what you are seeing or if you are over-restricting your observations to that which you wish to see. Further, you can ask how certain behaviors and events are related or disconnected or originated.

Having nonverbal visual representations of your site provides you with additional context, detail, and perspective. Using a similar process as the wide-angle lens, start in one part of the room and sketch various aspects of it. You do not need to capture the entire setting, but select "hot spots" or areas frequented by your participants, or draw the specific place in which one of your episodic vignettes took place. Consider frontal and bird's-eye views. Don't worry about your artistic prowess – the sketches help you see in new ways and may not necessarily be used for data presentation. You may also want to attach quotations you hear or significant phrases to each sketch, giving it a title that pushes your thinking. Artful depictions of your sites will also be invaluable reminders as you engage in your final data analysis and write up. You may want to hang them on your office walls to literally surround yourself with data.

As you think about your researching skills, consider your pattern of taking notes. There is a rhythm to observations, periods of intense notation followed by moments of contemplation and stillness. Don't worry about capturing every single second. Also, don't refrain from counting things. Just because you are doing qualitative research doesn't mean that a numerical value lacks in providing meaning. If you want to count how many times students raise their hands, or how often the teacher repeats a certain phrase, both examples within a certain time frame, then do it. Such information could be quite thought-provoking. But also remember that counting does not add greater validity to the study and one cannot generalize from occasional counting. Such counting is simply one more point of data.

Interviews, formal and informal

As with other forms of qualitative research, the participant interview is often a critical component of data collection. The goal of any participant interview, formal or informal, is to listen well. The researcher should ask specific questions seeking concrete examples that lead to detailed descriptions rather than vague speculations.

Conventional qualitative research wisdom tells us to tie our interview questions to our research questions and theoretical framework. This is a great place to begin. Further, if you are using Eisner's school ecology or the instructional arc, you may want to ask questions regarding the various appropriate elements. We also offer suggestions for types of questions appropriate to the educational critic.

The first is read and respond. It may be fruitful to read a brief and poignant vignette from your observation notes, and then ask the participant a follow-up question. For example, if you read the portion from the study of ecologically minded teachers (above) then you might ask, "I wondered about … " or "I noticed that … " or "I am curious about … could you tell me more?" Or even, "Is that how you intended the lesson to go?"

Second, you may want to select some aspect of the physical environment that stood out to you in your observations. Then, ask the participant to describe it in detail using his/her senses. You will want to listen for the connotations of the words used, the details included or omitted, the origin of the creation of the space, and other details pertinent to your study. Compare your own description to that of the participant and ask yourself questions about similarities and differences.

Having the right interview questions is an important start, but setting the stage for the interview ensures the questions receive their proper attention. The choice of venue for the interview may have an impact on the kind and quantity of ideas and information the participant is willing to share. If possible, ask him/her to select the space. It should be free of interruptions and should provide a space in which the participant feels able to speak openly. This may require an evening or "off" time meeting. Be sure to ask permission to record the interview, and do so each time you meet. Also remember to artfully describe the setting for the interview; all contexts are data rich.

Typing notes on a computer during an interview can be very distracting and may interfere with the kind of information shared. Begin with some informal and friendly discussion so that you are both at ease. Provide a copy of the interview guide to the participant so that she/he may jot down ideas and read the questions if desired.

One last word of advice: don't be afraid to ask challenging questions. But do be prepared to wait for responses or for the participant to muddle through an answer. Listen patiently.

Artifact collection

Artifacts are the "operational definition of what teachers value … indirect surrogates for values, expectations and behaviors that might otherwise be difficult to see and assess" notes Eisner (1998: 184). As such, artifacts such as lesson plans, handouts for students, curriculum binders, tools of the trade (staplers, smart boards, clay) become a part of the story the critic is telling.

Artifacts include any materials, documents, objects, photographs, teacher notes, student work, or available resources that are significant for your study, and available for your investigation (either to keep, to photograph, or to borrow). Their relevance depends upon the connections the researcher is able to make, which are in turn reflective of the researcher's perceptivity and imagination. On the importance of imagination in research, Eisner (1998) notes, "Information becomes data only if a researcher is able to make it meaningful" (p. 185). The researcher sees how otherwise disconnected parts coalesce to form the coherent story. Remember to include artifact collection in your Institutional Review Board permissions, and clarify if your use of photographs is strictly for data collection and analysis, or for use in publication. If you are collecting paper documents, you may want to make photocopies on which to directly record codes and notes so that the originals stay intact.

Once you have collected artifacts, it is important that they become an active part of your data collection. One strategy is to repeat the sensory experience, described above with observations, with the artifacts. Describe the artifacts in detail using all five senses, or one concentrated one. Ask questions about it – who created it? Why? For what other purposes might it be used? Must it look and feel this way? Infer some answers to your questions and generate further detailed descriptions and questions.

Another active strategy is to categorize what you collect in various ways. For example, you might categorize by creator (teacher, student, school, textbook company, community); by elements of Eisner's ecology (curriculum, pedagogy, intention, evaluation, structure); or by emergent theme. Then journal about how the categories help you understand the situation you are studying. Next, recategorize the artifacts and see what that yields. This should be done physically if possible, so pile the artifacts together.

Once you have a couple of sets of categories, ask the following questions:

- What do the categories reveal and conceal?
- How do the categories, and the artifacts arranged in such a way, inform your thinking?
- How do they relate to your observations and interviews?
- What emergent themes are appearing in all three data collection activities?

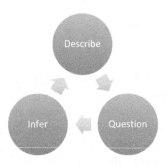

FIGURE 3.3 Inferring Meaning from Artifacts and Observations

An educational critic considers the reciprocal relationships between observations, interviews, and artifacts. Ongoing exploration of each element individually and as a group will help you refine your perception of the situation as you move toward interpretation and evaluation.

Reflective questions and activities

1. Practice interviewing a peer about his or her work as an educator. Determine in advance if you will take notes or/and record the interview. If you record the interview, practice transcribing a paragraph or two. What are the benefits and drawbacks of transcribing one's own interviews?
2. Review two dissertation proposals, one that employs educational criticism, and one that employs another qualitative method (such as ethnography, portraiture, etc.) Compare and contrast the proposals. What are the meaningful similarities and differences?

> Length of time at a site depends upon perceptivity. The classroom ecology consists of curriculum, pedagogy, school structure, evaluation along with teacher intentions and school–community relationships. Working relationships with participants may be viewed as deontological, utilitarian, caring, and ecological.

Note

1 It should be noted that Uhrmacher was not a connoisseur of Waldorf education when he began his study. His connoisseurship grew as he read immeasurably and as he conducted fieldwork. He also conducted pilot studies and visited several schools before his actual research began. Thus, we highly recommend that researchers consider doing a pilot study.

References

Barone, R. P. (2014). In search of social justice praxis: A critical examination of senior student affairs officers' leadership practices (doctoral dissertation). Retrieved from ProQuest Dissertations Publishing (3641961).

Berliner, D. C. (1988). *The development of expertise in pedagogy*. Washington, DC: AACTE Publications.

Conn, D. R. (2014). Attending to growth: Implications of the Colorado Growth Model for three rural schools (doctoral dissertation). Retrieved from ProQuest Dissertations Publishing (3644089).

Conrad, B. M. (2011). Intentions, operations, beliefs, dispositions of teachers at culturally diverse schools: Examining the intricacies and complexities of great teachers (doctoral dissertation). Retrieved from ProQuest Dissertations Publishing (3478277).

Crecinik, S. E. (1997). Levels of Acceptance of a teacher evaluation system based on Elliot Eisner's Educational Criticism and Connoisseurship Model (doctoral dissertation). Retrieved from ProQuest Dissertations Publishing (9806476).

Deleuze, G. and Guattari, F. (1987). *A thousand plateaus: Capitalism and schizophrenia.* London, UK: Continuum.

Denison, C. W. (1994). The children of EST: A study of the experience and perceived effects of a large group awareness training (The Forum) (doctoral dissertation). Retrieved from ProQuest Dissertations Publishing (9511962).

Eisner, E. W. (1998). *The enlightened eye: Qualitative inquiry and the enhancement of educational practice.* Upper Saddle River, NJ: Prentice Hall.

Flinders, D. J. (1992). In search of ethical guidance: Constructing a basis for dialogue. *Qualitative Studies in Education,* 5(2), 101–115.

Flinders, D. J. (1987). What teachers learn from teaching: Educational criticisms of instructional adaptation (doctoral dissertation). Retrieved from ProQuest Dissertations Publishing (8722994).

Ganus, L.A. (2010). The pedagogical role of Reggio-inspired studios in early childhood education (doctoral dissertation). Retrieved from ProQuest Dissertations Publishing (3398460).

Gutiérrez, J. (2014). Power of equality myths: A transdisciplinary study examining the influence of equality policy on teaching and learning (unpublished doctoral dissertation). University of Denver, Denver, CO.

Ingman, B. C. (2013). Rethinking the adventure education experience: An inquiry of meanings, culture and educational virtue (doctoral dissertation). Retrieved from ProQuest Dissertations Publishing (3588335).

Moroye, C. M. (2007). Greening our future: The practices of ecologically minded teachers (doctoral dissertation). Retrieved from ProQuest Dissertations Publishing (3253733).

Pryor, J. (2010) Constructing research questions: Focus, methodology, and theorization. In P. Thomson and M. Walker, *The Routledge doctoral student's companion: Getting to grips with research* (pp. 161–168). New York: Routledge.

Thornton, S. J. (1988). Curriculum consonance in United States history classrooms. *Journal of Curriculum and Supervision,* 3, 308–320.

Uhrmacher, P. B. (1991). Waldorf schools marching quietly unheard (doctoral dissertation). Retrieved from ProQuest Dissertations Publishing (9205736).

Uhrmacher, P. B. and J. Matthews (Eds.) (2005). *Intricate palette: Working the ideas of Elliot Eisner.* Columbus, OH: Pearson: Merrill Prentice Hall.

4

DESCRIPTION AND INTERPRETATION

Guiding questions

- How are description and interpretation used in educational criticism?
- What are the distinctions between description and interpretation?
- What is an interpretive frame? Can you provide some examples?

Introduction

In Chapter 1 we identified four dimensions of educational criticism: description, interpretation, evaluation, and thematics. This chapter will address the first two dimensions – description and interpretation. We begin with description because it represents a foundation for interpretation, evaluation, and the development of themes. The aim of description is to help readers see and hear what the critic has experienced. It seeks to engage readers by allowing them to situate themselves in relation to that experience. Description provides an account of events and situations experienced firsthand. In order to capture such experiences, the critic's use of description is often expressive in character. Interpretation explores the meanings of what the critic has described. In doing so, interpretation typically involves the critic's antecedent knowledge – analytic tools, models, interpretive frames, and theories – in order to extend descriptive data and link them to other work in the field. As such, interpretation overlaps with description. Critics and other researchers, for example, describe what they believe is worth describing, and this belief alone rests on conceptual assumptions and expectations.

However, description and interpretation each take a different emphasis, and their distinctive characteristics and aims are instructive for understanding the form and function of each. With respect to form, one useful distinction drawn from the teaching of writing is the difference between *showing* and *telling* writing. Showing writing expresses the qualities of a person, place, or event through firsthand examples and vivid accounts that are concrete and specific. Showing writing is descriptive. Telling writing attempts to explain the meaning of what has been observed. Its form is often abstract and propositional. Its function is to account for the qualities described by providing order, coherence, and structure. An educational critic, for example, may describe the chronology of a classroom lesson together with interview quotes describing the teacher's aims or intentions. The critic may then move into a more interpretive mode by addressing the relationship, in this case, between the intended and actualized curriculum. In Chapter 3 we called this the instructional arc. Thornton (1988) calls this relationship "curriculum consonance."

The distinctions we are making are also similar to a distinction originally used in linguistics (Schwandt, 1997) and later in anthropological and sociological case study research. This distinction is between an *emic* and *etic* perspective. The emic perspective reflects the research participants' point of view, what we earlier called "seeing with." The emic includes what Geertz (1983) called "local knowledge," or knowledge that is distinctive to a particular cultural group or local setting. Educational critics seek to portray local knowledge largely through description. This local knowledge is interpretive in the sense that participants make sense or "interpret" their own experience. But the critic's role in an emic approach is to describe, not theorize.

The etic perspective ("seeing about") represents the researchers' perspective, which is often the point of view of disciplined-based knowledge. It includes theories, concepts, language, and explanatory models often drawn from the critic-researchers training in the arts, humanities, or social sciences. In this sense, etic perspectives are forms of applied connoisseurship realized through interpretation. An etic perspective on standardized testing, for example, could be from the students' and teachers' perspective, and may include concepts such as distraction, chore, interruption, and perhaps for some, a guessing game. Mathison's (1993) early research on this topic took an etic perspective by focusing on what she terms "lay theories" (pp. 55–67). In her follow-up studies, however, she drew on anthropological concepts such as "ritual" to provide an emic perspective on the same phenomenon. She writes: "It is not difficult to demonstrate that standardized testing is a repetitive, stylized, performative act, one that is conducted by a designated person at regular intervals and that involves the manipulation of symbols. These are the essentials of a ritual" (p. 59). In listing some of the similarities between testing and other rituals, Mathison points to the "fit" between her focus (participants) and broader concepts. She also gains a set of analytic categories whereby each item on her list can be used to group or sort different types of data.

Description

Description serves at least two broad functions. First, it provides the evidence on which interpretations are built. This use of description, however, must come with a word of caution. The critic-researcher seeks to describe more than simply what he or she was looking for to begin with. Critics seek to describe what surprises them as well as what they anticipate. Moreover, it is rare for description, if done well, to fully support any single interpretation. Ideally, the critic is able to provide a rich or "thick" enough description for the reader to reasonably disagree with the critic's interpretations. Somewhat like literature, the text of a criticism must be open to different meanings for different people.

The second primary function of criticism is to contextualize a study's results. The importance of this function involves both the credibility and, as we will discuss in the next chapter, the generalizability of a study. Qualitative researchers at large have long recognized that their work is not statistically generalizable in a formal sense, arguing instead for naturalistic forms of generalizability under terms such as "transferability." Lincoln and Guba (1985) describe transferability as the "fit," relevance, or applicability between the context of the research and the context of its applications. Here generalizability follows the adage: "If the shoe fits, wear it." By contextualizing the study and its results, such description provides not only the size of the shoe, but also its color, style, and usefulness for different purposes. Again, we will say more about generalizability in Chapter 5.

If we turn from description's function to its form, it can be defined as a detailed, particularized and purposeful account of participants' social actions. As such, a "true" description is more than simply a collection of detailed facts. Rather, the critic seeks an expressive account, one that is expressive in the original sense of the term meaning "to press out" (see Dewey, 1934: 64). We view description as a form of pressing out of meaning. Its aim is not simply to depict, but to evoke images and to give the reader a visceral sense of places, people, and situations. Consider the following two examples. The first is a paragraph from Russel Baker's memoir *Growing Up* (1982):

> On a broiling afternoon when the men were away at work and all the women napped, I moved through majestic depths of silences, silences so immense I could hear the corn growing. Under these silences there was an orchestra of natural music playing notes no city child would ever hear. A certain cackle from the henhouse meant we had gained an egg. The creak of a porch swing told of a momentary breeze blowing across my grandmother's yard. Moving past Liz Virts's barn as quietly as an Indian, I could hear the swish of a horse's tail and knew the horseflies were out in strength. As I tiptoed along a mossy bank to surprise a frog, a faint splash told me the query had spotted me and slipped into the stream. Wandering among the sleeping houses, I learned that tin roofs crackled under the power of the sun, and when I tired and came back to my grandmother's house, I padded into the dark cool living room, lay flat on the floor, and listened to the hypnotic beat of her pendulum clock on the wall ticking the meaningless hours away.
>
> *(p. 58)*

This example gives a sense of what we mean by *particularized* description. Baker writes of "majestic depths of silences" and "natural music" by providing a string of specific examples. He also uses language – its rhythm and pacing – appropriate to the "hypnotic beat" of his grandmother's clock.

Our second example is from Sarah Lawrence-Lightfoot's *The Good High School* (1983). Her book describes six high schools; two urban, two suburban, and two "elite" high schools. Below is how she introduces St. Paul's, one of the elite schools.

The Aesthetics and Comforts of Abundance

It is a magnificent spring day. The sky is clear blue, the air crisp, and the sun golden in the sky. The landscape is lush green and the azaleas are exploding with blossoms of magenta, lavender, and deep orange. In short, it is the perfect day to visit St. Paul's School, which seems to stretch on for miles before me – aristocratic, manicured, perfect. I arrive midafternoon, the time for athletics, and see playing fields full of hockey and baseball players – lithe, graceful, and practiced bodies moving across the grass.

Everyone is helpful and welcoming. A man in a blue truck – probably one of the custodial crew – finds me lost on the road and tells me to follow him to my destination, the School House. Everyone waves greetings. A young man on a small tractor mower offers a wide, enthusiastic grin, and a tall, distinguished slightly graying man gives a stiff and formal wave. I park behind the School House, next to a car with windows open and a young child inside. Having just arrived from the city, I wonder immediately how anyone could feel safe about leaving a precious child in the car. Fearing that I will frighten her, I smile and speak softly to the little girl. She babbles back, unafraid. The child's mother returns after a couple of minutes. A plainly attractive woman of about thirty-five, she is one of the five females on the teaching faculty. She greets me warmly, introduces me to her daughter, and drives off quickly to play tennis. I am struck by how safe, secure, and beautiful it feels at St. Paul's. It is a place where windows and doors are left open, people exchange friendly greeting, and babies wait in cars unattended.

(p. 221)

These brief paragraphs function much like what in filmmaking is called an "establishing shot." Lawrence-Lightfoot orients her readers by taking them along with her as she arrives at St. Paul's, setting the stage for further description of people and events. Like Baker's paragraph, Lawrence-Lightfoot is particularized with specific examples. She does not simply tell us about St. Paul's, she shows us St. Paul's by describing its physical features and its aesthetic "tone." Then she uses this description to summarize her point that St. Paul's is, "a place where windows and doors are let open, people exchange friendly greetings, and babies wait in cars unattended." Also, like Baker, Lawrence-Lightfoot does more than simply present the facts. She also foreshadows and supports themes suggested in her title: "The Aesthetics and Comforts of Abundance."

Baker and Lawrence-Lightfoot's descriptions are similar in other ways as well. Both take the form of a brief chronology where one event follows the next. Each description tells a story. Baker's story could be titled, "When the Men Were Away," and Lightfoot's might be titled, "Arriving at St. Paul's." Each provides a miniature narrative of events as they happened. Chronologies and narratives are common ways to organize descriptive material, allowing the critic to invite readers into a particular setting, develop characters (participants), and use their actions to develop the story's plot. At a more fundamental level, narratives lend coherence to the critic's direct experience and understanding. As such, they are a primary and focal way in which humans make meaning.

Interpretation

As we noted at the beginning of this chapter, it is often difficult to draw a hard and clear line between description and interpretation. In a well-crafted educational criticism, description and interpretation fit hand in glove. The degree to which description goes beyond a simple recounting of events to support or foreshadow themes, relationships, and concepts is the degree to which description overlaps with interpretation. The difference in emphasis between the two is largely a matter of the critic's aims. Eisner (1991) put it this way: "If description can be thought of as a giving an account *of*, interpretation can be regarded as accounting *for*" (p. 95, emphasis in original). This "accounting for" seeks to explicate the meanings of descriptive data by providing some type of conceptual order or structure.

We define interpretation as the application of concepts, often through the use of analyses and metaphor, in ways that foreground the relationships, patterns, or reasons for events and situations at hand (one's data). Interpretation is a search for meaning and a way of seeing. As such, it has a long history in the humanities, social sciences, and especially in approaches to qualitative research. Hermeneutics is an example. This philosophical grounding, which is used in a range of qualitative studies (including some educational criticisms), originated as an approach to translating and interpreting ancient and sacred texts such as the Bible. While other examples abound, even qualitative research as a whole has at times been conducted under the labels of "interpretive" or "interpretivist" inquiry, labels that suggest the central role of interpretation across qualitative approaches. Likewise, Schwandt (1997: 73–74) argues that this interpretive focus is a way to distinguish the purposes of qualitative inquiry (understanding) from the propositional, law-like causal explanations sought in the physical sciences.

Other qualitative approaches often distinguish between a conceptual and a theoretical framework. For example, Egbert and Sanden (2014: 5) suggest that a conceptual framework is located with the researcher herself; it is "an overall worldview … an individual perspective defined not only by values and perceptions (Northcutt and McCoy, 2004), but also by the sum of one's experiences, beliefs, and knowledge from every facet of life, including, for example, gender, religious, family, political, social, academic, and environmental arenas." They go on to argue that a conceptual framework is the "integration of the theoretical concepts that apply to the problem under investigation," (p. 60). Because of the integrative nature of connoisseurship and criticism, we use the term *interpretive frame* to be inclusive of both the researcher's point of view as well as the theories she applies to the situation.

Mathison's (1993) approach to standardized testing illustrates the aim of understanding (as opposed to control). She began with lay theories and moved to social theories in order to link her participants' views to the shared meanings of her research community. She describes the origins of her research as rooted in her surprise to find testing such a prevalent practice in US schools compared with her own experiences in Canada. Educational critics often begin with a thesis or a broad question (Why is standardized testing so prevalent?) that remains open throughout the study. We will offer a second example that illustrates a similar pattern. This example is from art criticism (see Eisner, 1985). Like Mathison, the paragraphs below by critic Leo Steinberg (1966) blend description and interpretation, almost seamlessly integrating the two. Below are the first few paragraphs of Steinberg's review of a retrospective exhibition of Paul Brach's paintings.

FIGURE 4.1 *Paul Brach: Whole #1 (1962) (oil on canvas, 45 x 40 inches)*
Source: image courtesy of © Cordier and Ekstrom, Inc., New York.

Paul Brach's Pictures

They are very near invisibility.

Invisibility is of various kinds, and to list its varieties while the pictures are up helps to focus attention.

Invisibility by disappearance. An object absent, remote, or indistinct leaves a leftover emptiness and a straining to see. This seems relevant to Brach's pictures. Their vacant geometry suggests depleted voids, voided containers. Their huge suspended circles can look like extinguished suns. Solar cult emblems snuffed out. Empty icons.

Then invisibility by extinction of light. This too seems relevant. Not actual darkness – which conveys a specific degree of absence of light – but a consistency or opacity that can be neither brightened nor deepened.

And invisibility due to dimmed vision; whether through blindness or the sightlessness of inattention. Brach makes his pictures easy to resist. They court unseeing indifference or disinterest, as if to remain invisible to the averted mind.

(in Eisner, 1985: 228)

Steinberg begins with what can be read as a thesis: "They are very near invisibility." This statement paves the way for more fully interpretive sentences such as: "Brach makes his pictures easy to resist." The critic's second sentence, "Invisibility is of various kinds, and to list its varieties while the pictures are up helps focus attention" is an analytic move to identify "kinds" or types of invisibility. Steinberg also uses this sentence to state his purpose – to focus attention. His varieties of invisibility are a way to structure and organize of the qualities of Brach's paintings that the critic has experienced and seeks to help his readers understand. Readers might also sense a playfulness, and perhaps irony, in Steinberg's approach. Even invisibility can be used as a way of seeing.

We also want to note how the critic's language parallels the qualities of the work he is describing. The first paragraph is a single, five-word sentence. Like Brach's "empty icons," the sentence hangs alone, pared down to a simple, brief abstraction. Other sentences also seem clipped and minimal. "Invisibility by disappearance," stands as its own sentence, and without an action word, it seems almost inert and remote, again reflecting the qualities of the paintings that the critic has experienced. Even the title, "Paul Brach's Pictures," expresses this minimalist style. An English teacher might take issue with Steinberg's sentence fragments and deliberate transgression of paragraphing conventions, but his writing works, given its particular context of a Brach retrospective. That is, it works for what the critic seeks to convey. The review is descriptive, but descriptive with a purpose.

Interpretive frames

While Steinberg chose invisibility to frame his review as appropriate to the paintings at hand, he might have selected other frames around which to organize his criticism. Other concepts associated with abstract expressionism, such as sub-conscious expression or Jungian analysis, could have offered a different focus. Our point is that different interpretive frames yield different questions, perspectives, and lessons to be learned. We will illustrate this point with another example that draws on three different frames.

Julie is a science education doctoral student. Through her earlier teaching in environmental education, she became interested in "intergenerational knowledge," an idea drawn from eco-justice scholarship. Intergenerational knowledge is represented in face-to-face, cross-generational learning in non-formal settings. Environmental authors such as Bowers (2006, 2014) have argued that intergenerational knowledge is less abstract and less monetized than print or digital communication. Drawing on local sources, intergenerational knowledge also contributes to more ecologically sustainable lifestyles. As Julie's interests grew, she began asking people informally for examples of something they had learned from an elder through firsthand interactions. She noticed that responses tended to fall into two categories. Some people offered examples of concrete, practical skills; one person, for instance, recalled his grandfather teaching him as a child to tie his shoes. Another person mentioned that her mother taught her how to can food. Others responded with much more general "lessons," such as when people told Julie, "My aunt taught me the importance of self-respect," or "My father taught me to be honest."

In Julie's later work she would raise questions about the relationship between these two seemingly different but related response types. Julie also framed intergenerational knowledge as a part of the "commons," another concept drawn from eco-justice scholarship. Doing so not only provided her with an interpretive grounding for further study, it also helped her sharpen her focus, formulate appropriate research questions, and connect her study with other eco-justice research.

While Julie decided on an eco-justice frame for these purposes, she could have chosen another interpretive frame. Had she drawn on critical theory, Julie would have likely used other concepts than she did. Critical theory, rooted in the historical viewpoints of Karl Marx and Friedrich Engels, focuses on socioeconomic status, inequality, the reproduction of social hierarchies, and the exploitation of labor in industrial capitalist countries. In education, critical theorists worry that schools offer the most opportunities to the most advantaged, and the least opportunities to the least advantaged. They also worry that the commodification of labor leads to teacher or student self-alienation and false consciousness. In this approach, however, workers (such as students and teachers) are not simply viewed as pawns in the production of goods. Instead, they may actively resist alienating conditions and relationships.

Even this brief description suggests that critical theory places intergenerational knowledge in a different light than does an eco-justice frame, thereby raising different research questions. What is the relationship between intergenerational knowledge and social class or economic standing? Julie and critical theorists may well share points of interest, such as on the social status of knowledge, and here the two frame-works overlap somewhat. Still, the concepts used to define status differences, such as class reproduction and resistance, would likely distinguish a critical theory perspective from many other frames of reference. How does intergenerational knowledge, for example, contribute to class reproduction? In other words, who benefits from intergenerational knowledge? The least advantaged may benefit if or when intergenerational knowledge is employed as a form of resistance against commodification (eco-justice scholars would use the term "enclosure") of the spoken word and of other aspects of local community building.

Julie might have sought still another interpretive frame by drawing on the work of feminist scholars. We cannot present the full range of possibilities in taking this approach or the nuanced differences among various concepts. But we can note that feminist scholars usually share an abiding interest in gendered experience and gender equality, raising the question of how women's intergenerational knowledge differs from that of men. This interest in equality again overlaps with an eco-justice and critical theory perspective. Yet, this shared interest does not diminish the distinctive concepts and lines of inquiry suggested by feminist thought. For example, Julie could have used Noddings' (2005, 2013) work on caring and the ethics of care as her basis for interpretation. Noddings approaches caring not as an individual trait or virtue, but as a relationship among two or more individuals. Without going into details, care theory places an emphasis on interpersonal relationships that promote confirmation, modeling, and opportunities for guiding the practice of caring. Here again we have another set of questions. What is the relationship between caring and intergenerational knowledge? How do modeling, confirmation, and guided practice contribute to intergenerational knowledge, or vice versa?

Criteria for interpretation

Julie's example leaves us with three different frameworks, and we could easily add more. Which frame – eco-justice, critical theory, or care theory – is the correct choice? And how do educational critics decide? "Correct" in this context has neither a single answer, nor is it a matter of capital "T" truth. All three of Julie's options may be a correct choice, provided they are relevant to her study, provide help in conceptualizing her research, and suggest how to make sense of the results. This is an important point about the uses of interpretation. As we have been arguing, different interpretive frames offer different ways of seeing, and each may be of value. Still, different educational critics, like many other researchers, may be drawn to particular theories or frames. Our question is why this is the case, or what makes some interpretations more useful than others. The overall aims of interpretation are to bring meaning, order, or structure to otherwise desperate or poorly understood aspects of an experience. This aim suggests two pertinent criteria: relevance and conceptual power.

With respect to relevance, this criterion depends on the particulars (purposes, rationale, participants, etc.) of a given educational criticism. The significance of these particulars again underscores the role of vivid descriptions of the experience or phenomena at hand. The critic seeks an interpretation that best "fits" these particulars. We have just suggested that the particulars of a criticism serve as a basis for interpretation, but making this determination may also draw on the critic's own experience and levels of connoisseurship within a particular domain. Multiple frames may be used in some criticisms, but we argue below for balance and restraint to guard against using so much interpretation that the overall focus and coherence of the criticism suffers. A little interpretation goes a long way.

Thus, judgments must still be made, and critics may face a situation where multiple interpretations seem equally relevant. In such cases, questions surrounding the conceptual power of an interpretive frame are central. By conceptual power, we mean the capacity of an interpretation to explicate or explain the critic's observations. Does the interpretation serve as a guide to understanding? Does it illuminate or bring into focus aspects of an experience that might otherwise go unrecognized? Does it position or juxtapose dimensions of that experience in ways that make sense? Does it help us make the strange familiar or the familiar strange? What are the implications of an interpretation for improving educational practice, policy, or theory? As these questions imply, the conceptual power of an interpretive frame is closely linked to evaluating the usefulness of the work as a whole.

Conclusion

In this chapter we have examined the roles of description and interpretation in educational criticism. While we have considered each of these dimensions of criticism as separate topics, they overlap and in many cases are inseparable. Description guides the critic's interpretations, and vice versa. In concluding, we will briefly highlight our main points about the uses of description and interpretation. We also suggest the need for balance.

The use of description in this context goes beyond a stripped-down, objective statement of the facts of the case. Critics and other researchers are obligated to be as accurate as possible in recounting information, but the facts alone do not speak for themselves. If description is sterile and detached, it is neither a "true" description in the sense of true to one's experience, nor is it likely to aid understanding. Because the critic's descriptive aims are to invite and engage readers in the process of learning to see and hear, description in educational criticism seeks to be vivid and expressive. As our examples from Russell Baker's childhood and Sarah Lawrence-Lightfoot's study of St. Paul's High School illustrate, expressive description has the potential to represent the tone and feel of a particular place, as well as its other nuanced qualities. Expressive description places an experience in its context, allowing readers themselves to build meaning from that context.

Interpretation is a heuristic that critic-researchers use to organize, structure, and connect descriptive data to larger ideas. As such, it requires more inferential thinking than does description. Interpretation is a search for patterns and relationships suggested by whatever concepts, theories, or models that the critic finds relevant and useful for explaining the meanings of social actions. It is a way to get beneath the surface of routine and often taken-for-granted behaviors by asking the seemingly simple question: What is going on here? But, again, while interpretation is informed by what people do and say, its focus is on what these doings and sayings mean. What do they signify, symbolizes, or represent? We continue to pursue such questions in the next chapter by focusing on two further dimensions of criticism: evaluation and thematics.

Before turning to these topics, however, we want to mention that critics may have individual styles and leanings that emphasize one of these dimensions – either description or interpretation – over the other. While the balance between the two is ultimately a matter of judgment, we should not disregard the distinctive functions of each. Description without interpretation risks leaving one's readers wondering what the point of description is to begin with. On the other hand, interpretation without description may lack credibility or any basis for judging the interpretation's relevance and value. Description-"lite" criticism risks showing too little and telling too much, a problem suggested by Sir Winston Churchill when he said, "I am always ready to learn, although I do not always like being taught."

Reflective questions and activities

1. Using your observations from Chapter 2, describe what you observed in an artful way. Practice using literary yet honest language. Next, interpret this description in at least three ways by placing your description in a larger context.
2. Find several examples of critiques. You may want to explore movie reviews, local art show write-ups, or other topics of interest. Consider how the critic's review informs the way in which you understand and come to know the object of critique. In what ways is the art critic's work similar to that of an educational critic, and in what ways is the work different?

For proposals and doctoral dissertations, your methods section of your docu-
ment should have several paragraphs about description and interpretation.
Inform the reader about the importance of description, and also discuss your
interpretive frames.

References

Baker, R. (1982). *Growing up*. New York: Penguin Putnam.

Bowers, C. A. (2006). *Revitalizing the commons: Cultural and educational sites of resistance and affirmation*. Lanham, MD: Lexington Books.

Bowers, C. A. (2014). *The false promises of the digital revolution: How computers transform education, work, and international development in ways that are ecologically unsustainable*. New York: Peter Lang.

Dewey, J. (1934). *Art as experience*. New York: NY: Perigee.

Egbert, J. and Sanden, S. (2014). *Foundations of education research: Understanding theoretical components*. New York: Routledge.

Eisner, E. W. (1985). *The educational imagination: On the design and evaluation of school programs* (2nd ed.). New York: Macmillan.

Eisner, E. W. (1991). *The enlightened eye: Qualitative inquiry and the enhancement of educational practice*. New York: Macmillan.

Geertz, C. (1983). *Local knowledge: Further essays in interpretive anthropology*. New York: Basic Books.

Lawrence-Lightfoot, S. (1983). *The good high school: Portraits of character and culture*. New York: Basic Books.

Mathison, S. (1993). From practice to theory to practice. In *Theory and concepts in qualitative research: Perspectives from the field*. David J. Flinders and Geoffrey Mills (Eds.). New York: Teachers College Press, pp. 55–67.

Noddings, N. (2005). *The challenge to care in schools*. New York: Teachers College Press.

Noddings, N. (2013). *Caring: A relational approach to ethics and moral education* (2nd ed.). Berkeley, CA: University of California Press.

Northcutt, N. and McCoy, D. (2004). *Interactive qualitative analysis: A systems method for qualitative research*. Thousand Oaks, CA: Sage.

Schwandt, T. (1997). *Dictionary of qualitative research terms*. London, UK: Sage.

Steinberg, L. (1966). Paul Brach's pictures. In G. Battock (Ed.), *The new art: A critical anthology* (pp. 226–228). New York: Dutton.

Thornton, S. J. (1988). Curriculum consonance in United States' history classrooms. *Journal of Curriculum and Supervision*, 3, 308–320.

5

EVALUATION AND THEMATICS

Guiding questions

- What are the aims of educational evaluation?
- Who is the audience for such evaluations?
- What does it mean to "generalize" from an educational criticism?
- How does one defend one's work in relation to issues of subjectivity and validity?

Introduction

Evaluation and thematics provide the audience with the "upshot" of the educational situation explored by the researcher, and ways to anticipate features of similar situations. Evaluation focuses on appraisal of the educational experiences in relationship to a set of criteria in a particular context. Chapter 5 explores various criteria that are appropriate for use in evaluation, and we distinguish between criteria and standards. We also offer several types of curriculum (intended, operational, received, hidden, complementary, null, and shadow) as points of focus for a critic in conducting the evaluation.

We present thematics as a process of sense-making through identifying and describing "pervasive qualities" (Eisner, 1998) of the situation described. Such themes allow us to anticipate, as a form of generalization, similar features in different contexts. We argue that what one may learn from one school or classroom provides anticipatory frameworks that help us understand other educational contexts and the general educational enterprise. We provide the basis for validity, discussed as consensual validation, as established through structural corroboration and referential adequacy, and suggest various tools for achieving trustworthiness through strong design.

Evaluation and thematics

The juxtaposition of evaluation and thematics provides the researcher and her audience with two salient areas of consideration: the evaluation, in which the researcher articulates her appraisal of the object of study, and the themes, in which she provides an anticipatory framework with which to guide subsequent appraisals of similar contexts, situations, or phenomena. In this way, the educational critic both provides educative and valuable information for the immediate participants, as well as findings that may be carried into other situations and used as initial lenses for observation and appraisal.

As such, we first discuss the meaning and function of evaluation, followed by an exploration of the ways in which themes may be derived and for what purpose. We then explore issues of validity as appropriate to this research method.

Evaluation

As Eisner (2002) pointed out, there are many functions of evaluation. From a diagnosis, to program comparisons, to determining whether objectives have been met, contemporary education is rife with evaluation and assessment. We wish to immediately distinguish between the kinds of assessments commonly given and the type of evaluations educational critics perform.

First, in simple terms, when educators today refer to assessment, they generally mean in relationship to some pre-specified criteria. Contemporary educational assessments tend to be for the purpose of "temperature taking" and as indicators of successful progress toward a goal. Whether criterion- or norm-referenced tests, common assessment practices seek to show how a particular student or group of students is performing based upon a predetermined set of standards.

When we refer to evaluation, however, the educational critic asks what is of value here, both for those involved and for the educational enterprise generally speaking? The purpose of an evaluation is to assess the significance of events in relationship to a set of criteria, not solely to measure them against an external standard, although that may be a part of the overall picture. While many current assessments tend to strip away "superfluous" aspects of the schooling experience to hone in on skills learned, the educational critic embraces the intricate details and their meanings. As Eisner (2002) so poignantly reminds us, "the denial of complexity, in educational matters, as in politics, is the beginning of tyranny. Educational criticism could contribute to the appreciation of such complexity and therefore provide a more adequate basis for the making of educational judgments" (p. 233). The educational criticism not only explores and honors the complexity, but it also may lead to a deeper appreciation for such intricate workings while informing decision-making.

Evaluation, in this way, can account for, and can indeed help us see and understand, the well-documented unpredictable nature of classrooms and schools (Jackson, 1990). Both assessments and critical evaluations can help educators make decisions and improve the lives of students. The educational critic, however, points out unexpected or idiosyncratic but noteworthy phenomenon.

Educational criticism's clear intent "is to improve the educational process" (Eisner, 2002: 233) through judgment of the situation based upon educational criteria. The critic, keeping her own values and biases in mind, provides an appraisal that references a pertinent set of criteria, such as Dewey's framework for educative experiences.

To elaborate upon one example of educational criteria, we briefly discuss, as Eisner did, Dewey's (1938) criteria for an educative experience. Dewey argued that there are three types of experiences to be had in education: educative, miseducative, and non-educative. An educative experience, said Dewey, is characterized by continuity and interaction. Continuity refers to the qualities of an experience that meaningfully connect to students' lives and which lead toward growth. Interaction refers to the balance between student's internal conditions with the external conditions of the situation or content. Together, "continuity and interaction in their active union with each other provide the measure of the educative significance and value of an experience" (Dewey, [1938] 1997: 44–45). A non-educative experience has no bearing or consequence on the growth and development of humans; it simply is not a significant learning moment but is not necessarily harmful. However, a miseducative experience hinders growth both in the present and possibly future contexts.

We provide the brief overview of Deweyan criteria for educational experience as a way to consider how a general educational framework can inform the perceptions of the critic. The criteria are general enough to be meaningful in a variety of contexts without overly limiting the researcher's perception and ability to see meaningfully. And, because the criteria are directly related to qualities of an educative experience, an appraisal with such criteria in mind has the potential to improve the educational lives of students.

It may also be useful for the critic to have additional salient points of focus that may be utilized with her conceptual framework, which the critic may have at hand at the earliest stages of the research process. One example includes the various types of curriculum, including the intended (Eisner, 2002), operational (Eisner, 2002), received (Venezky, 1992), hidden (Jackson, 1990), complementary (Moroye, 2009), null (Flinders et al., 1986), and shadow (Uhrmacher, 1997).

Although these ideas may be woven into the research questions themselves (see Chapter 3), they also may serve as guideposts in emerging appraisals. For example, an educational situation may be strongly influenced by the structure of the classroom, its decorative features, furniture, and posted materials and messages. Such physical characteristics may pervade the educational situation without being directly addressed or spoken about by the participants, but to the educational critic, exploring the meaning of the hidden curriculum of the physical environment may yield significant findings. Similarly, the educational critic may notice that the teacher's beliefs about a non-instructional event or experience may influence his instruction. For example, a teacher who believes in and values art may infuse his science class

TABLE 5.1 Types of Curricula

Intended	That which is formally or informally determined (by a teacher or other authority) to be taught. "The course of study; it is that which is planned. Such plans can … be inspected, critiqued, revised, and transported to a multitude of locations." (Eisner, 2002, p. 32)
Operational	That which actually is taught. "The operational curriculum is the unique set of events that transpire within a classroom. It is what occurs between teachers and students and between students and students. To critique or appraise the operational curriculum requires one to be in a position to observe what classroom activities actually unfold." (Eisner, 2002: 32–33)
Received	That which students learn and experience, whether intended or unintended. (Venezky, 1992: 439–440)
Hidden	The ways in which classroom life informs social norms and expectations, as well as patterns of behavior that are routinely practiced but seldom scrutinized as curriculum features. "The crowds, the praise, and the power that combine to give a distinctive flavor to classroom life collectively form a hidden curriculum which each student (and teacher) must master if he is to make his way satisfactorily through the school" (Jackson, 1990: 33–34)
Null	That which is not taught, which has been left out or removed from the curriculum. "What schools do not teach" (Flinders et al., 1986: 33)
Shadow	The "dark side" of a curriculum that may be unearthed through reflection on "what the curriculum privileges and what it disdains." (Uhrmacher, 1997, p. 318)
Complementary	The intentional or unintentional expression of a teacher's beliefs. "The kinds of experiences teachers provide for students, as well as in the 'pedagogical premises and practices' that result from the teachers' beliefs." (Moroye, 2009, p. 791)

with artistic materials, may often draw spontaneous connections between art and science, and may create aesthetically pleasing classroom materials. Exploring this teacher's beliefs through the complementary curriculum may yield a deeper understanding of how the teacher orchestrates rich learning environments for students and/or how he engages students differently.

Another set of readily available criteria for such an appraisal includes various curriculum theories (or ideologies). While such theories can inform the entire educational criticism, they may provide various criteria by which the critic forms judgments during the evaluative process.

As noted in Chapter 4, the educational critic may explain the major features of a classroom or school through the lens of the theory or ideology. For example, if a teacher is working toward a goal of student engagement and he tends to use direct

TABLE 5.2 Curriculum Ideologies

Rational humanists	The best education for the best is the best education for all. Expose students to the best of Western culture.
Developmentalists	Cognitive structures develop naturally. If the setting is right, students will raise questions and push their own thinking.
Reconceptualists	One learns through experience. We can understand experience through phenomenology, psychoanalysis, and literature.
Critical theorists	A just society maximizes the advantage for the least advantaged. Schools must be analyzed as part of the larger community and society.
Multiculturalists	Students' ethnic identities should be embraced and included in the school curriculum and pedagogy.
Cognitive pluralists	Students learn about and construct meaning through sensory experiences.
Ecologists	Humans' relationships with the natural world should be explored throughout school curriculum.

Source: adapted from Uhrmacher (1997).

instruction and recall methods, the critic might appraise the situation for its essentialist qualities and then offer ideas from progressive or existentialist theories that may enhance the engagement in the classroom. The skilled critic may also contribute to the theories themselves, adding elements or examples that further deepen or elaborate upon the theory itself.

But what makes an evaluation meaningful? How does unearthing complexity and highlighting idiosyncratic qualities improve the educational enterprise? Coming from the pragmatist perspective, an educational criticism is meaningful insofar as it is valuable to the intended audience. The critic discerns meanings *with* and *about* the various stakeholders in terms of a set of educational criteria that provide a useful lens and heuristic for thinking about educational practices. To do so the educational critic wants to "see with" and "see about." Or, to again borrow terms from ethnography, the educational critic utilizes both emic and etic points of view in order to discern meaning for those involved, as well as by providing fresh eyes to see and offer recommendations or ways of considering the situation.

It is important to note that the educational criticism is not a "truth" in the sense that it is the only way to account for or to interpret a situation. Rather, the criticism provides one way to look at and understand the educational situation. It may be that another critic would appraise the situation quite differently.

Because the critic's evaluation is informed by her own beliefs and values, it may be useful to clearly articulate such beliefs in a "critical prologue" (Eisner, 2002: 232), which is analogous to writing about one's "positionality" or "researcher bias" in other qualitative approaches. Such an explanation of beliefs and values, while perhaps abundantly clear in the write up of the criticism, allows the reader to contextualize the criticism in terms of the critic's belief system; the reader may consider the background of the researcher in determining if the criticism is useful and on target.

Before moving onto thematics, a word of advice about how to think about evaluation in terms of the research process. As we mentioned earlier, the researcher is likely to go into the setting with prefigured and emergent foci (see Chapter 3). Prefigured means that one has some ideas in mind as to what to look for; emergent means that the critic will allow the setting to influence her ideas and that she remains open in terms of how to interpret and evaluate the setting until the middle or even the end of observations. Our ideas about the various kinds of curriculum and theories can be utilized upfront as prefigured. In this scenario, the critic has already decided that she will look at her setting in terms of a specific theory, for example. Perhaps she has decided to focus on pragmatic race theory. In this case, she might look for educational and miseducational opportunities and misfortunes. She might also use the various curriculum terms mentioned above as a way to evaluate the setting when she is in the midst of her observations. If, however, the researcher decided to rely on an emergent focus, then she may utilize these ideas at the tail end of the research process. One may still evaluate the setting using the ideas above, but such ideas will come in the data analysis stage after observations have been conducted. In either case, we wish to emphasize that Dewey's ideas about education and miseducation, the different kinds of curricula (received, hidden, etc.) and the curriculum ideologies may all be used alongside the ecology of schooling and the instructional arc as mentioned in Chapter 3. That is, these ideas may be built into those frameworks and/or be utilized independently.

Thematics

Recalling that evaluation provides an appraisal from the educational critic's perspective, thematics, the fourth dimension of an educational criticism, articulates the patterns, big ideas, and anticipatory frameworks for other educational situations. The themes distill the major ideas that run through general educational matters and provide guidance, not a guarantee or prediction, for understanding broader educational contexts. In Eisner's (2002) words, "What does it all add up to?" (p. 233).

Thematics is analogous to other forms of generalization in qualitative research, therefore, we first provide a brief discussion of generalization before moving into the process of data analysis as described through coding and what we call *annotation*. We then discuss the process of moving codes and annotations to themes that serve as anticipatory frameworks before finishing with a discussion of validity.

Generalizations: transferability, schema theory, and anticipatory frameworks

The decades-long debate over validity and generalization in qualitative research continues. From Wolcott's (1990) rejection of the need for validity in qualitative research to Lincoln and Guba's (1985) criteria for appraising qualitative research, the spectrum of beliefs still influences qualitative methodologies.

Lincoln and Guba (1985) describe four evaluative criteria for trustworthiness of a qualitative study: credibility, transferability, dependability, and confirmability. Trustworthiness is a conglomeration of these qualities that demonstrate the "truth" of the findings – that they are applicable in other contexts, that they are consistent, and that the findings are not unduly influenced by the researcher.

To achieve trustworthiness, the researcher has many options, such as prolonged engagement, persistent observation, triangulation, peer debriefing, referential adequacy, and member-checking (Lincoln and Guba, 1985). Such techniques may lead to what Lincoln and Guba (1985) call *transferability*, rather than generalization, and are applied with consideration for the new context, rather than a blanket prediction for all contexts. Donmoyer (1990) takes the notion of transferability to new ground, suggesting that researchers need fresh language to talk about the ways in which qualitative research can be meaningful in contexts other than the particular study site.

Donmoyer (1990) argues for a view of generalizability "rooted in a conception of experiential knowledge" (p. 186) that is adequate for portraying the experience of individuals. He proposes the use of *schema theory* and Piaget's notions of assimilation, accommodation, integration, and differentiation. These cognitive processes describe the ways in which research provides the audience with a vicarious experience that takes on meaning to the individual engaged with reading the work. The reader filters the research data, connects it to his own experiences and ascribes meaning, which may or may not be the same in all cases.

Echoing Barone's (2000) conception of aesthetic inquiry, the evaluator, or in our case the educational critic, discerns meaning for and with the stakeholders and significance in terms of educational criteria for participants as well as for the educational enterprise. An educational critic, then, thinks about generalization in the sense that we are drawing "inferences from a sample" (Eisner, 2002: 236).

Eisner (2002) argues for two types of generalization that arise from educational criticisms. The first is a more "refined process of perception" (p. 242) cultivated by and for the educational critic herself. The more she practices the art of perception, the more of a connoisseur she becomes; "skills generalize" (p. 242). The second type of generalization is described as the "creation of new forms of anticipation" (p. 242). Such anticipatory frameworks are created by the critic's perception and articulation of the particulars of a situation, and then held up against the backdrop of the larger educational context. These particulars, presented as themes, may be applied to new situations. The critic curates her "repertoire of anticipatory images" (p. 242) and shares them with others by allowing us to appreciate the uniqueness of a situation along with its significance for others.

The creation of anticipatory frameworks is a significant component of the role of the critic, as it supports her work toward educational improvement. For example, Trousas (2009) in her study of arts-based reforms asked, "What are the aims of arts-centered school reformers in the two schools studied?" (p. ii). In her discussion of themes, she begins with a succinct statement of her findings: "Arts-centered school reform exists as a menagerie of educational experiences created through the artistry of teachers," (p. 334). She then notes two main categories for the teachers' aims: holistic vision and collaboration. She elaborates on the theme of holistic vision saying, "Teachers embrace a holistic vision of learning and childhood that balance students' experiences in arts-centered schools," (p. 334). She explains collaboration in this way: "Teachers share a commitment to creating a collaborative culture for students in arts-centered schools."

Such themes and "naturalistic generalizations" (Eisner, 2002: 233) may guide our future perception. Having Trousas' themes of holistic and collaborative aims in mind, the educational critic may view other schools or educational contexts for such instances. However, it is important to note that critics' and educators' future perceptions should not be narrowed by recognition of such themes, but rather the themes serve as entry points for further deepened seeing and elaboration upon the ideas.

Coding data

The generation of the themes is an on-going iterative process that may begin, as with other forms of qualitative research, by coding data. Many methods for coding data and attending to emergent themes are readily available. Glesne (1999) recommends beginning the "rudimentary" (p. 132) coding process once the data collection begins. Naming and categorizing types of data and ideas as they are collected gives the researcher a way to see the priorities and emergent patterns. Codes may be adapted and subdivided as more data are collected. Because the educational critic may not observe over extended periods of time, it may be important to begin the coding process early in the study. Conversely, depending upon the research questions, it may be important to allow data to remain unnamed for a period of time so as not to interfere with perception. If the researcher is skilled in remaining open to *seeing* rather than *recognizing*, coding early is recommended. For additional ideas and coding procedures, we recommend Saldana's *The Coding Manual for Qualitative Researchers* (2009), which explores 29 coding methods.

In educational criticism, coding is an interpretive act, the "transitional process" (Saldana, 2009: 5) between data collection and analysis; the names themselves have meaning. Because educational critics have an eye toward aesthetic perception, it may be useful to select interesting and artful names for the codes and, ultimately, the themes. As Glesne (1999) suggests, once data are collected and the organization and analysis processes get going, asking a set of questions about the data will help significant codes emerge: "What is being illuminated? How do the stories connect? What themes and patterns give shape to your data?" (p. 135). The educational critic may also ask about the salient features of the physical environment and the relationships between the elements of the school ecology (intentions, curriculum, pedagogy, structures, evaluation, school-community relations) as discussed in Chapter 3. This ongoing process of questioning the data leads to the creation of themes and anticipatory frameworks.

Annotation as an alternative to coding

We note that coding stems from the sciences; it is a term used in genetics, computer science, as well as the social sciences. The idea of a code is to transmit a meaning often in found in secretive formats. Coding qualitative data can take on a technical character, one that isolates phrases, counts their occurrence, and takes meaning from frequencies. While codes are one way for critics to view and analyze data, we also suggest perspectives from the arts and humanities. A literary critic, for example, does not usually talk about coding a poem or a text, but rather annotation. Educational criticism, rooted in the arts, may offer an alternative to coding that, rather than isolating phrases, focuses on the relationship among them in a complete picture. Consider the ways in which literary critics analyze poetry. Rather than code, they annotate the text often beginning by looking at the voice, tone, speaker, diction, syntax, imagery, and other features common to all poems. The purpose of annotating various elements is to then offer a new way of seeing the poem as an interconnected whole.

An educational critic, then, may annotate the vignettes or other descriptions that have emerged in their data collection. To do so, we might follow the lead of the literary critic and begin by reading the description aloud several times, attending to rhythm, dialogue, interactions among participants and the environment, various kinds of curriculum at play, and other salient features found in most educational situations. By considering them in a complete picture, we can then analyze the relationships between the common features of a classroom (or other setting) that make the space unique and meaningful for its inhabitants. The annotations may then be refined and moved toward anticipatory frameworks and themes, just as is done through the coding process.

While we are comfortable with a less structured manner of annotating the data, we know that some students of the method like to have specific processes that they can follow. We refrain from overly prescribing techniques in part because we believe that each setting deserves the researcher's full perceptivity – not an attention to formula. Still we know that some researchers want a language they can use to articulate their methods to others. Thus, we offer three types of annotations that the critic may perform. These include: global annotations, pattern-finding annotations, and cross-checking annotations.

Global annotations remind the critic to examine the data at-large. Look over the entire data set to see what stands out, to discern important contours of the situation and experiences of those involved. Pattern-finding annotations point the critic to look for configurations of meaning. In this phase, the researcher looks at the data set for more refined themes. Cross-checking annotations encourage the researcher to look for what some might call discrepant case analysis. That is, look for data that do not fit your themes. If there are too many data, then it may be the case that there are further themes for you to find. But if there are only some data, that may be an expected outcome due to the fluid nature of schools and social contexts. Eisner once put it this way: "it should be recognized that most situations about which an educational criticism is written will not be crystal clear or unambiguous; most of life is riddled with dilemmas, trade-offs, ambiguities" (Eisner, 1998: 111).

From coding/annotating to thematics

Similar to Saldana's explanation that categories are larger buckets in which codes may be sorted, thematics are the larger buckets given names that hold significance and are supported by the various codes, annotations, and related data. In Moroye's (2009) study, "classroom interactions" was a code that emerged early on. As the relationships between teacher and student, along with the ways in which the teachers fostered relationships among students, became increasingly significant, the code "classroom interactions" then informed the theory of "ecological caring," which is described as "the system of caring relationships at work in a classroom, which stem from and promote an ethic of care encompassing three central areas: care for self; care for others near and far (human and nonhuman); and care for plants, animals, and the earth" (Moroye and Ingman, 2013: 599). Later, in the final research report, the codes and themes became titles of the vignettes.

If working with a research team or partner, the process of coding can be collaborative or it may begin individually and then become shared and discussed for comparison and contrast. In a recent study of aesthetic themes in lesson planning, Conrad et al. (2015) explored how teachers could enliven their curriculum planning by using aesthetic themes of connections, risk-taking, imagination, sensory experience, perceptivity, and active engagement (CRISPA). Conrad facilitated a workshop on the CRISPA themes, and then Moroye and Uhrmacher analyzed the data. As a part of the educational criticism, they explain their collaborative research process:

> After the workshop, the other two researchers, Moroye and Uhrmacher, independently and then collaboratively analyzed the 14 watercolors and the transcript of the focus group discussion. Similar to the process outlined by Saldana (2009), we conducted two rounds of coding culminating in a third round of categorization and then subsequent thematic findings. The First Cycle (Saldana, 2009) coding consisted of independent descriptive codes focused on the experiences of the participants as portrayed through their comments during the focus group and the watercolors they created. We used such nomenclature as "lesson planning" and "experience of teacher" and "experience for students." We identified instances of corroboration and dissidence between the participants' verbal and visual representations of their experiences. In other words, we did not rely upon our own interpretations of the participants' drawings. Rather, we used the combination of their comments about their work with the images they created to more deeply perceive what the workshop meant to them. The Second Cycle (Saldana, 2009) coding, conducted jointly by Moroye and Uhrmacher, began with a comparison of our independent codes and resulted in refined categories of planning experiences: attention to the student experience,

creativity, and professional transformation. From the categories, the data took shape in the form of four thematic findings, which then informed our theory of disruption.

(p. 7)

Validity

Eisner, echoing Dewey, argues that we "construct our conception of reality by interacting with the environment" (2002: 236). This construction is influenced by past experiences, beliefs, and expectations. Eisner further argues:

> Objectivity is a function of intersubjective agreement among a community of believers. What we can productively ask of a set of ideas is not whether it is *really* true but whether it is useful, whether it allows one to do one's work more effectively, whether it enables one to perceive the phenomenon in more complex and subtle ways, whether it expands one's intelligence in dealing with important problems.
>
> *(p. 237)*

From this pragmatic perspective arises the ways in which an educational criticism may be interrogated for validity. In order to reach consensual validation, or the state of shared belief, an educational criticism must demonstrate structural corroboration and referential adequacy.

Structural corroboration

Structural corroboration may be described as the presence of a coherent, persuasive whole picture. The data collected and presented validate each other; the story makes sense. Multiple kinds of data from different participants may be examined for recurrent behaviors, patterns, and even the absence of certain qualities. It is also important to consider idiosyncratic or disconfirming evidence and to ask questions about the presence of anomalies.

The structurally sound criticism is characterized by consistency and coherence and deftly portrays the situation supported by evidence for the critic's impressions. Direct quotations, dialogue, rich description, and specific details paint the picture. Of course, as was alluded to above, the criticism is not likely to be "picture-perfect" because life itself is not. Further, the researcher achieves structural corroboration by checking the ongoing observational or other data against each other as well as her initial impressions.

Referential adequacy

The second aspect of validity for educational criticism is referential adequacy. Is the criticism useful? Does the critic's work indeed allow the audience (teacher, community, other researchers and educators) to see education in a new way and for purposes deemed important? Referential adequacy is achieved through member checking, interview questions dealing with the significance of the topic, and attending to contemporary and historical trends in education. The critic provides guideposts, such as in a travel guide, for those exploring educational terrain. Thus, not a single definitive criticism stands to tell the "truth" about a situation, but rather, the criticism could be one of many.

In summary, as we explore evaluation and thematics together, we may think of evaluation as the critic appraising the value for those involved. Thematics, the counterpart to evaluation, then offers shared particulars that open up anticipatory frameworks for other educational contexts. In order for the evaluation and thematics to hold up, to achieve consensual validation, they must demonstrate structural corroboration and referential adequacy.

Reflection questions and activities

1. Review an educational criticism and reflect upon the evaluation and themes provided. What kind of anticipatory framework does the researcher provide? How might it help you understand or appreciate or explore another educational situation?
2. What does it mean to you to demonstrate trustworthiness in your study?

Through evaluation and thematics, educational critics seek to provide anticipatory frameworks that may be utilized to understand educational situations and to support the improvement of educational practices.

References

Barone, T. (2000). *Aesthetics, politics, and educational inquiry: Essays and examples*. New York: Peter Lang.

Conrad, B., Moroye, C. M., and Uhrmacher, P. B. (2015). Curriculum disruption: A vision for new practices in teaching and learning. *Current Issues in Education*, 18(3).

Dewey, J. ([1938] 1997). *Experience and education*. New York: Simon & Schuster.

Donmoyer, R. (1990). Generalizability and the single case study. In Eisner and Peshkin (Eds.), *Qualitative inquiry in education: The continuing debate* (pp. 175–199).

Eisner, E. (1998). *The enlightened eye: Qualitative inquiry and the enhancement of educational practice*. Upper Saddle River, NJ: Prentice Hall.

Eisner, E. W. (2002). *The educational imagination: On the design and evaluation of school programs*. Upper Saddle River, NJ: Prentice Hall.

Eisner, E. W. and Peshkin, A. (Eds.) (1990). *Qualitative inquiry in education: The continuing debate* (pp. 121–152). New York: Teachers College Press.

Flinders, D. J., Noddings, N., and Thornton, S. J. (1986). The null curriculum: Its theoretical basis and practical implications. *Curriculum Inquiry*, 16(1), 33–42.

Glesne, C. (1999). *Becoming qualitative researchers: An introduction* (2nd ed.). New York: Longman.

Jackson, P. W. (1990). *Life in classrooms*. New York: Teachers College Press.

Lincoln, Y. S. and Guba, E. G. (1985). *Naturalistic inquiry*. Beverly Hills, CA: Sage.

Moroye, C. M. (2009). Complementary curriculum: The work of ecologically minded teachers. *Journal of Curriculum Studies*, 41(6), 789–811.

Moroye, C. M. and Ingman, B. C. (2013). Ecological mindedness across the curriculum. *Curriculum Inquiry*, 43(5), 588–612.

Saldana, J. (2009). *The coding manual for qualitative researchers*. London, UK: Sage.

Trousas, C. A. (2009). Teacher artistry and the not-so-still life of arts-centered school reform. (unpublished doctoral dissertation). University of Denver, Denver, CO.

Uhrmacher, P. B. (1997). The curriculum shadow. *Curriculum Inquiry*, 27(3), 317–329.

Venezky, R. L. (1992). Textbooks in schools and society. In Philip W. Jackson (Ed.), *Handbook of research on curriculum* (pp. 436–461). New York: Macmillan.

Wolcott, H. (1990). On seeking – and rejecting – validity in qualitative research. In Eisner and Peshkin (Eds.), *Qualitative inquiry in education: The continuing debate* (pp. 201–232).

6

TRENDS AND VARIATIONS

Guiding questions

- Can educational criticism be utilized in non-educational settings?
- How has educational criticism been adapted and modified over the years?
- What lessons can educational critics learn from literary and art critics?
- What holds for the future of educational criticism?

Introduction

In this chapter we delve into a number of ideas, each of which broadens out the way in which we may think about educational criticism and connoisseurship. The first is that educational criticism, as it has been conceptualized and developed in education, may be applied to studies of non-educational environments. Students in all fields, including, but not limited to, psychology, business, nursing, and social work will want to take notice. Second, we offer ideas about how one might adapt ideas found in educational criticism to allow for varying methodological tools. Third, the educational critic's imagination may be sparked by understanding some of the developments in literary criticism, in particular. We offer a number of ideas for fodder that may advance one's thinking about interpretive frameworks. Finally, critics may wish to explore the ways in which educational criticism may complement other research methods. We will take a look at some possibilities at the end of the chapter.

Criticism and connoisseurship

In the same way that Elliot Eisner conceptualized and developed educational criticism and connoisseurship by adapting ideas from the arts and humanities, researchers in fields outside of education may choose to borrow these educational ideas and apply them to their areas of study. In fact, some have already done so. Allow us to provide an example in order that the reader can see how such studies may take shape.

Charles Denison, for example, as we pointed out in Chapter 3, a student of counseling psychology, applied the ideas of criticism to a large group awareness training called The Forum, a derivative of Erhard Seminars Training (EST). Denison's dissertation (1994), titled "The Children of EST: A Study of the Experience and Perceived Effects of a Large Group Awareness Training (The Forum)," asked the following research questions: "What are the conditions provided in The Forum, and what is the process that is experienced under those conditions? What is the effect (outcome) of the experience, as perceived by the individual participant?" (p. 52). Denison conducted 20 interviews and attended several Forum trainings.

Denison, in our view, clearly helps the reader feel as though he is actually at a Forum event. Allow us to quote at some length:

> The mood is light and friendly. Darcy's big smile and energetic demeanor hold the attention of this diverse group. The 10-inch elevated platform seems too confining for Darcy, and she steps down closer to the 150 men and women gathered here.
>
> Few of us seem to know what is going to happen over the next three days so most listen carefully, hoping some light will be shed in this windowless room. The casual atmosphere in the room is formalized only by flawless rows of lightly-padded, straight-backed chairs ...
>
> Darcy, our leader, has welcomed us and assured us that the weekend will be life-changing, full of 'breakthroughs.' The beaming faces of the volunteer 'assistants' in the back of the room seem to affirm her promises.
>
> "OK, how many of you were pressured to be here?" Darcy casually asks. She is standing even with the first-row center, right hand in the air to model the method for responding to the question. Still smiling – "Go ahead and just raise your hand if you were pressured to be here." Nine or ten hands go up over the next five seconds.
>
> "OK, great! Now those of you who raised your hands stand up." Pause. Half a dozen slowly stand. "Come on now, go ahead and stand up if you were raising your hand. Who was pressured to be here?" A bit more movement; now eight are standing. "Okay, great, thank you," Darcy acknowledges them. "That wasn't so bad."
>
> Her facial expression now becomes more serious, and a tone of authority is projected in Darcy's voice: "Now, those of you who are standing, you want to just make your way to the table in the back of the room there. Please take off your name tags and give them to Sharon. Then Randall will give you your $290 back including your $50 deposit. You are dismissed and you can leave and go on about your weekend." The Forum has begun!

In a matter of thirty seconds, the room has undergone a transformation of mood. All jocularity has taken its leave. The silence of the participants seems to ask, "Now what?"

(pp. 1–2)

Denison deftly interweaves two voices: the narrator and Darcy's. Through the narrator's voice, the reader experiences the change from a light mood to a serious one. Denison tells us at the start that the mood is light and friendly; he backs up his statement by detailing Darcy's smile. But then the narrator takes us through a series of events by quoting Darcy, who changes the mood of the room through her words toward those who felt pressured to be at The Forum. Toward the end of the above paragraphs, the narrator says, "The Forum has begun," and "Now what?" which tells the reader that we are in the thick of the Forum experience and reflects the reader's question about what happens next.

As we mentioned earlier in this book, it is important that researchers inform the readers a little about their background and biases – what some researchers call subjectivity (Eisner and Peshkin, 1990) or positionality (Lincoln, 1995). At this point, one may wonder whether Denison has "gone native." But Denison tells us that "there is much that I do not, personally, like about the organization which presents The Forum" (1994, p. 234). He believes, for example, that it is too profit-driven. But he also believes that the philosophy of The Forum is "healthy, tolerant and altruistic" (p. 234). He states, "Irrational beliefs were often challenged in the training" (p. 234). The Forum is not a psychological cure, but Denison believes "[Irvin] Yalom's 'therapeutic factors of group psychotherapy' are present in the process of The Forum" (p. 235). And he adds that in an age in which "mental health service strategies are changing rapidly" (p. 235), there is much to be learned here. Thus, the other rhetorical move to notice is that Denison ties his research into something larger – in this case, what in other places in the dissertation he calls LGATs (Large Group Awareness Trainings) – and to the scholarly literature – see Yalom's (1985) *The Theory and Practice of Group Psychotherapy*, for instance.

We offered the example of Denison's dissertation so that readers can learn some of the details in adapting educational criticism. Now we provide some general recommendations for researchers who wish to adapt educational criticism for non-educational settings. First, note that any environment that has some kind of intention behind it, in our view, immediately becomes a possible subject for criticism and connoisseurship. The number of sites for critics to study is endless. They include schools, colleges, museums, large and small businesses, hospitals, therapy sessions, online programs, and even landscapes such as national parks and sports facilities. Any researcher interested in understanding the intentions behind a particular environment, inquiring into how the environment actually functions, and what may be done to improve it may be interested in utilizing criticism and connoisseurship.

Second, we have already discussed the matter of connoisseurship earlier in this book. Thus, in addition to the above criteria for choosing educational criticism, the researcher should also have an interest in placing him or herself on the connoisseurship continuum with the desire to increase one's expertise. The researcher ought to have firsthand experience in the field, a growing knowledge base, and a sense of what criteria are important for understanding excellence within a given context. So, for the educational critic, experiences and expertise in education are needed; for medical or environmental studies, knowledge and expertise in those areas are required.

Third, and this is easy, drop the word "educational" from the method's title. The method may be called criticism and connoisseurship and could be referred to as such in proposals, dissertations, and published articles. The author should note that the ideas employed were derived from Eisner's works, or this book, or some other text in the field of education. As we indicated in Chapter 1 and will elaborate upon below, there are many types of criticism. Researchers embracing these particular ideas need to delineate the tradition within which their studies are to be found.

Adaptations

Most qualitative research traditions undergo modifications as researchers use them. This is true in part because, generally speaking, qualitative researchers are more interested in using a method to assist in uncovering some aspect of the world than they are in remaining faithful to a prescribed manner of conducting research. Qualitative research, in order to be responsive to the context, is often messy and improvised. It has been said, for example, that there are as many ways to do grounded theory research as there are grounded theory researchers. In our view, those who have chosen educational criticism and connoisseurship have not diverged too much from Elliot Eisner's prescriptions. For the most part, educational critics have described, interpreted, evaluated, and thematicized their work. But, having said that, there have been variations on the method, and we believe there are more to come. Allow us to mention a few that we have found thought-provoking. These include revising Eisner's ecology, providing summative rather than observational descriptions, and juxtaposing educational criticism as a complementary method to other qualitative methods.

Revising the ecology

To begin, researchers may want to consider Elliot Eisner's ecology of schooling and adapt its framework to fit other settings. We discussed this idea in Chapter 3. Denison, referring to the example above, used and modified Eisner's (1994) ecology of schooling (see Chapter 3) as a framework to guide his observations and interviews. He defined curriculum as the content that was transferred between Forum leaders and participants; pedagogy became the manner in which the content was delivered; and school structure became simply structure, in this case referring to how time and space were utilized by Forum officials. Since it was not useful, Denison dropped the category of evaluation. Uhrmacher added the category of aesthetics (1991) to Eisner's ecology, and later he and Matthews (2005) added school/classroom–community relationships. One might add other dimensions related to the study site or field as well. Cloninger, for example, added administration to the framework (2008). The main point is that whatever is added needs to be integral to the framework so that the effects of changing one dimension do indeed affect each of the others. We also note that one could delete dimensions. We have taken intentions out of the framework and placed it in the instructional arc. If a researcher did not plan on looking at evaluation, as another example, one might delete that dimension from the ecology. This is not to say that the dimensions, once removed from the ecology, are no longer an integral part of the whole. But, rather, the researcher is paying particular attention to specific ecological elements and drawing attention to their features.

Summative description

Another adaption that we have seen is modifying what we may call observational (or attendant) description from the four-step method of description, interpretation, evaluation, and thematics. Attendant description means the kinds of descriptions found in most current educational criticism books and articles: sentences, paragraphs, and pages dedicated to representing what one observed in a setting. Sometimes, however, due to the nature of the study and/or access and design issues, researchers do not conduct observations. In these cases, it is not paramount that one stays focused on the idea that educational criticism necessitates observation and observational description. In lieu of observation, the researcher may provide summative rather than attendant descriptions. Kristen Bunn (2009) utilized an engagement measure as well as educational criticism. Rich Patterson (1997), as another example, used a survey to respond to the following research questions: What are the intentions of the primary stakeholders who are concerned with Artists in Residence in the state of Colorado? What are the teachers' perceptions of the impact of the Artists in Residence Program? What is the significance of the Artists in Residence program for arts education in general? To answer his questions, Patterson employed the ecology of schooling framework – including the category of aesthetics – and he interpreted, evaluated, and created themes. While Patterson did not conduct observations, we do wish to point out that he had a type of description, which for the moment we may call non-literary. The survey data is, however, a type of portrayal and as such is a type of description.

Educational criticism as a complementary method

Carolyn Mears (2005) asked the question, "What is the experience of parents of students who have been exposed to a rampage school shooting?" and utilized educational criticism and oral history. According to Mears, "Oral history has provided the means of collecting the parents' reflections on their life experiences, and elements of educational criticism and connoisseurship have been adapted for reporting the results" (p. 51). As with the dissertation mentioned above, Mears did not conduct observations. But she did report her interview data through poetic representations, noting that poetry brings the reader closer to the participants and it also adds to the emotional context. Says Mears, "As a result, the data become more alive and accessible than they might in extended paraphrases or prose summaries" (p. 59).[1]

Another dissertation that refrained from classroom observations was that of Lorry Getz (1997), who studied how independent schools perceived state educational standards. Similar to Patterson's dissertation, Getz utilized survey data. But while he did not describe schools or classrooms in a traditional sense, he did describe his experiences with interviews. That is, he informs the reader what the school looks like and he describes his entrance to meet with school leaders. Here is one example:

> When I arrived at School Six, the sun was shining and you could hear birds singing. I pulled into the parking lot and behind a group of light brown church buildings was a long brown school building. To the left were some temporary classrooms and a walkway that led up to the main entrance.
>
> I looked around the main entrance of the school and was surprised to see little student work or projects. There was very little to indicate that this was a school. ... From behind me, I heard a door open and a voice say, "Please send these out today; they need them at the other school as soon as possible." I turned to see a heavy set man with a dark suit talking to his secretary. He turned to look at me and a smile spread across his face. He raised his hand to shake and he said, "You must be Mr. Getz, come on in."
>
> I started the interview by asking Mr. Peters what his role in the school was. "Well I'm the administrator, the classification is superintendent. The idea was to start four Christian schools on the four sides of the city and a metro high school."
>
> *(pp. 248–249)*

Through this style of description of the interviewee along with direct quotations, the reader gets a feel for the actual people as well as their words.

Finally, Heather Beck (2003), in her study of nontraditional superintendents, also provides readers with some description to lead into and break up participants' interview data. We will refrain from citing her conversations with participants whom she met face to face, but here we note one interview that was conducted over the phone. After providing interview data, Beck writes: "As I listen to Mr. Holmes over the telephone, I cannot but wonder what he is doing while we are on the phone. Is he watching TV or looking through a magazine? Is he looking out a window? He speaks in a slow, methodical manner with many long pauses and breaks" (p. 66).

These kinds of descriptions do more than simply break up the interview data; they also provide a feel for location or for the character of the participant or of the interviewer or both. As such, they add layers of meaning whereby the reader may make sense of the data overall.

We note that elements of educational criticism may be utilized with almost any other qualitative research method. Carrie Vanderbrook (2005), for example, attempted to combine educational criticism with phenomenology. As complementary methods, researchers may be attracted to any number of devices and arguments employed by educational critics and, subsequently, they should not refrain from using them even if their own work is not situated within the educational criticism tradition. As Eisner (1991) once noted,

> How is a researcher to take events occurring in real time and reduce them into what Lightfoot (1983) calls 'a portrait' and what I call an educational criticism of what the observer – in my case, the educational connoisseur – has experienced? This is a task of storytelling, and in the telling of any story, theme, plot, and point are important considerations.
>
> *(p. 189)*

In general, qualitative researchers pay attention to these aspects of their work and, as such, remain closely tied.

Looking to literary criticism's past for fresh directions

To begin our examination of new directions for educational criticism, let's look once again in more depth at the meaning of the word criticism and the role of the critic. Our discussion focuses on literary criticism in particular, but we must point out that literary and art criticisms have many commonalities. Moreover, when we look at some current theories such as deconstructionism, theory and philosophy often co-mingle. Authors such as Derrida are not easily placed in one disciplinary camp, and the ideas he, and others such as Foucault have developed, are cross-disciplinary endeavors.

But we are getting ahead of ourselves. Let's start by looking to the past, especially ideas that are not salient, and in doing so we will note opportunities for the future. As we pointed out in Chapter 1, the term criticism emerged in the English language in the early 1600s to refer to the Aristotelian idea of "a standard of judging well" (Welleck, 1981: 298), but it was not until Alexander Pope's (1711) "Essay on Criticism" that the term would be solidified – at least in England. The essay argued for both the importance of the critic as well as how "he" may go about his work. The first stanza below attests to the importance, while the second (which comes later in the essay), suggests that standards for taste stem from nature herself:

> Both must alike from Heav'n derive their Light,
> These born to Judge, as well as those to Write.
> Let such teach others who themselves excell,
> And censure freely who have written well.
> Authors are partial to their Wit, 'tis true,
> But are not Criticks to their Judgment too?

Those RULES of old discover'd, not devis'd,
Are Nature still, but Nature Methodiz'd;
Nature, like Liberty, is but restrain'd
By the same Laws which first herself ordain'd.

Thus, one early goal of criticism was to create standards of judgment. Today, we spend less time on seeking objective standards for judgment, but we would note that some of the recent brain-based research aims at finding a biological basis for our conduct, actions, and even thoughts.

Moreover, the idea found in the first stanza of the poem of having a standard of judgment has persisted. In sports competitions such as ice-skating for example, the judges seek to reduce the variability in responses to what they have seen. Judges choose to agree on what jumps, spins, and rotations are important and then on how each move ought to appear. By reducing variability on judgment, the goal is to select the best skater given specific criteria. The same kind of goal is found in the field of education in any standardized test one has created or endured. We know from personal communication that Eisner himself resisted the idea of utilizing several researchers to corroborate uniformity of opinion; rather, he believed that each researcher ought to employ his or her own sensibilities to "see" and to help others "see" what otherwise might go unnoticed. To use an analogy, we do not need two film critics to come up with the same ideas about a film; much more interesting is what each film critic individually will reveal. Thus, one new direction for educational criticism is to have several critics observe a school setting, not with the goal of coming to consensus, for the reasons just mentioned, but to reveal the complexity of teaching by highlighting what each critic believes is important.

While much was subsequently written and developed around Aristotle and Pope's goals for standards of judgment, German philosopher and poet Johann Gottfried Herder (1774–1803) broke with that tradition. Herder's thinking was that "in order to understand and interpret a piece of literature is to put oneself in the spirit of the piece itself" (Welleck, 1981: 300). According to Herder, "It is 'the natural method, which leaves each flower in its place, and contemplates it there just as it is, according to time and kind'" (p. 300). From Herder's perspective, works of art achieve their function by becoming part of a larger milieu, much like an individual plant becomes part of an environmental landscape. Thus, under Herder's influence, "literary study became a kind of botany" (p. 300). While not personally familiar with Herder's argument back in 1990, Uhrmacher (1991) used this type of rationale for his study of Waldorf schools. That is, one reason for studying Waldorf education was that any and all types of alternative types of schools ought to be studied for their own sake. This overall argument, in our view, still stands. Researchers in their chosen fields ought to find and understand the overall varied terrain of their fields of study. In the field of education, critics ought to pursue and understand all of the varieties that fit under this appellation.

Johann Goethe (1749–1832), a polymath writer and student of Herder's, distinguished two kinds of criticism: destructive and productive. The nomenclature itself informs us of Goethe's bias. On the one hand, destructive criticism is "simply the application of a yardstick" (Welleck, 1981: 300) – preformed ideas. On the other hand, productive criticism asks the following kinds of questions: What did the author set out to do? Was his plan reasonable and sensible, and how far did he succeed in carrying it out? Says Welleck, "Goethe hopes that such criticism may be of assistance to an author and admits that his own criticism describes largely the influence which books have had on himself" (p. 300). Goethe's hope also, in our view, applies to the ways in which critics may help practitioners in their field. In fact, this very idea was taken up in the 1980s by those involved in clinical supervision and an early essay by Eisner (1982) speaks to these issues. Educational criticism could and should assist educators in practical ways. After reading a criticism, teachers, for example, may be able to see themselves in new ways and learn how to improve.

Finally, a word about poet and philosopher Friedrich Schlegel (1772–1829), who noted that criticism must "'ascertain the value and non-value of poetic works of art'" (Welleck, 1981: 301). It can be done, he argued, by paying close attention to the text, which must begin with an intuition of the whole of art history. According to Schlegel, every artist illuminates every other artist and together they form an order. "The critic must 'reconstruct, perceive, and characterize the subtle peculiarities of a whole'" (p. 301). But, says Schlegel, criticism also has another function: "polemics, incitory, anticipatory criticism, a criticism which would be not merely explanatory and conservative, but productive, by guidance and instigation stimulating an emergent literature" (p. 302). We will leave it to others to discuss the influence Schlegel had on postmodern critics, but we point out that his observation that criticism can be "incitory" and "stimulating" to something new is in line with much current thinking that criticism is about creating new modes of thought (see Colebrook, 2002). How Schlegel may view current postmodern writing is debatable, but we believe his call for new modes of thought is in line with what today we would call postmodern discourse (see Best and Kellner, 1991). What this means for educational critics and practitioners alike is that they might consider new forms of thinking about education with new ways of presenting their information. We note that this is exactly what takes place in several venues at the American Educational Research Association's annual conference. Readers may wish to look at the Elliot Eisner Special Interest Group (SIG) and the Arts-Based Research SIG.

Our look at past discussions around criticism is admittedly idiosyncratic and partial. Neglected in our discussion, for example, are Matthew Arnold, Henry James, and F. R. Leavis, among many others. As much as we have left out the far past (1800s), there is even more that we must leave out from the near past (1900s) and present. Arguably, there have been at least 12 major developments each deserving of attention. These include: new criticism, critical theory, structuralism, post-structuralism, reader–response theory, psychoanalytic criticism, feminism, postmodernism, postcolonialism, deconstruction, and the new historicism. Each of these positions on criticism has much to offer critics. By bringing various lenses to bear on the object of interest, each one has the opportunity to uncover new ideas and actions. Nonetheless, we will refrain from describing each of these intellectual movements. For one, doing so would add about another 100 pages to this text, which is not something we can provide. Moreover, there are already some very good overviews of these types of theories/criticism. We refer the reader to Terry Eagleton (1983), Steven Best and Douglas Kellner (1991), Charles Bressler (1999), and Peter Barry (2009) as just a few places one might begin to focus on these various movements.

We will, however, make a few broad-stroke observations about these theories and then we will elaborate on three theories that do not make the larger headlines and which we believe deserve greater attention. These include ecocriticism, pragmatic race theory, and the new aesthetic criticism. All of these theories are ones that may impact the researcher's lens for data collection and analysis.

A variety of theories

To begin, we wish to provide a few reflections on the recent theories that have come into play since the mid-nineteenth century. To help make sense of it all, we would note that the various literary theories highlight or downplay different aspects of the following statement: *A situated (intended or not) object of focus that yields meaning.* We make the statement quite abstract so that it may be applied to a variety of fields, from nursing to educational criticism. In any field, however, we note that each of the theories we mention may be employed as the researcher's interpretive framework, thereby affecting data collection, analysis, and write-up. Let's examine the statement's various aspects in order to understand how criticism has changed its foci over time.

By "situated," we mean that the object of focus, which is not necessarily a literal physical object, can be examined in contexts outside the object. A novel such as Ralph Ellison's (1995) *Invisible Man* can, for example, be examined by focusing on the author's intended meaning (Goethe's constructive criticism) of the text or the author's unintended meanings (psychoanalytic approach). In addition, one may write extensively about the text in its historical (new historicism) or cultural (cultural criticism) contexts. One may also view the text as a symbol or signifier in a chain of other texts (structuralism) and be more concerned with how it reveals underlying aspects of mind, narrative, or the cosmos. Finally, situated could also refer to the ways in which the text is part of a larger system of values promulgated by materialism and capital interests (critical theory) and/or race (critical race theory).

The "object of focus," as we already mentioned, does not necessarily mean a physical object, though it could refer to something like a statue. More often than not, object of focus refers to the center of the study, which may be anything from a novel or a poem to a classroom or a school. Some would argue that the situated aspects of the object are irrelevant (new criticism) and that all which is needed is a focus and study on the object itself. In the field of literary criticism, the "new critics" argued that a poem is like a "Grecian Urn" and has an ontological status not unlike an actual physical object. Today, however, many would temper that argument by suggesting that indeed the focus may be on a text, but to display its relevant meaning fully, an examination of the historical context is important too (new historicism).

Finally, we need to understand the last part of the statement, "that yields meaning." By this, we refer to the fact that the object of focus is the cause of a discussion about meaning (all of the theories) and/or where meaning resides (postmodernism). Reader–response theorists focus on the process whereby the reader creates meaning. Post-structuralists and postmodernists might note that there isn't *a meaning* from a text, but rather numerous meanings, each of which may have some validity. Deconstructionists, as perhaps a subset of postmodernity, might focus on the fact that meanings will always shift and change and that any stable meaning is likely to be cause for suspicion in that in its frozen aspect it points to interest groups who have a stake in one particular kind of meaning.

Obviously, this brief overview cannot do justice to the full and rich discussions that have taken place under each of the orientations previously mentioned, and in its simplicity it overlooks complex ideas that cannot be easily boxed. It does point out that theorists over time have largely focused on one or several of the elements distinguished in this one statement and, as such, the statement has utility in helping one understand the current field at large.

Moreover, and this is our second reflection on the various theories, a student of the field would do well to recognize that each intellectual movement has to some degree reacted to past movements and created a new trajectory of thought. The new critics, for example, were tired of philological studies and argued that a text stood for itself; nothing outside the text was needed to create meaning. Of course, reacting to this orientation were those who sought to understand a text in its relationships to other texts (structuralists), to a superstructure that set on a base (Marxist brand of critical theory), or to a superstructure that is independent of a base (Althusserian style of critical theory).

Third, we must note that each intellectual movement continues to grow. While a particular idea such as deconstructionism may have been initiated largely by one writer, in this case, Derrida, we would note that deconstructionism as a label may fit a variety of efforts, from literary theorists de Man and Culler to Spivak and Johnson. Similarly, there are numerous ways to do and think about structuralism. It is not the case that there is only one version. In addition, sometimes an orientation has great popularity for a while and then grows into disfavor (new criticism for example). Nonetheless, an older orientation, as we will show below, can be fitted with correctives and then grow again (see aesthetic criticism).

Summing up, we provided this overview as a way to think about numerous theories that have currency and widespread applicability. Each of the approaches mentioned above has been applied to education philosophically and each has been utilized by one researcher or another as a framework to understand an educational context (see Morrell, 2004, and the book series published by Peter Lang, called Counterpoints: Studies in the Postmodern Theory of Education). Educational

TABLE 6.1 Literary Theories

New criticism	Close reading of a text without an examination of the author's intentions or the historical period in which it was written
Critical theory	Examination of a text in terms of production and reception in relation to matters of socioeconomic class in particular
Structuralism	Reading of a text for its underlying structure and its relation to a universal interpretive framework
Post-structuralism	A decentering of the text such that any passage may be read in multiple ways and no version represents the "right" one
Reader–response theory	A focus on the ways in which readers make sense of the text
Psychoanalytic criticism	A focus on the author's psychological make-up and/or psychoanalytic themes found within the text
Feminism	An examination of representations of women in a text or in a genre
Postmodernism	Often a playful mix of literary genres in which even the criticism plays a role
Postcolonialism	An examination of imperialism and diversity, or the lack thereof
New historicism	An interpretation of literature based on non-literary texts, with a continual juxtaposition of the two

critics may choose one of the theories as a way to understand an educational environment. A summary of some major theories is listed below. Keep in mind, however, that each theory may contain numerous approaches. There isn't just one way to do critical theory, for example; there are probably a dozen or more.

Ecocriticism

As we mentioned, it would take too much space to elaborate on each of the major literary movements that have been popular in the last half century. We also noted that there are other texts that provide excellent overviews. There are, however, several orientations that have not received a great deal of attention, which we believe are important and deserving of mention because their utility extends beyond literature. As we also mentioned in the last section, each theory may prove useful in guiding one's interpretive framework and hence data collection and analysis. We start with ecocriticism.

Ecocriticism, also called environmental or green criticism, in large part draws attention to the environment and the human relationship with it. Says Garrard (2012) "Ecocriticism explores the ways in which we imagine and portray the relationship between humans and the environments in all areas of cultural production, from Wordsworth and Thoreau through Google Earth, J. M. Coetzee and Werner Herzog's Grizzly Man" (p. 3). Just as feminist criticism calls attention to gender, and Marxist criticism highlights economic class, ecocriticism privileges the understanding of environmental ideas and portrayals.

Such relationships between humans and the environment can be analyzed through the story itself, diction, character, and other literary elements. Just as David Orr (1992) argues that all education is environmental education, due to the lessons learned by what is included and ignored about the earth, all literature may be considered "environmental" in the sense that it may be analyzed through an ecological lens. This may be especially interesting in texts and classrooms in which the ecological ideas or relationships are concealed or implicit; the critic's role is to surface such details and interpret their significance. In this way, ecocriticism is "an avowedly political mode of analysis" (Garrard, 2012: 3).

Barry (2009) points out that ecocritics attend to "green" concepts such as "growth and energy, balance and imbalance, symbiosis and mutuality, and sustainable or unsustainable uses of energy and resources" (p. 254). And while they may read any text from an ecological perspective, they focus upon nature writers, such as the American transcendentalists, as well as giving new space to relevant 'factual' writing, especially reflective topographical material such as essays, travel writing, memoirs, and regional literature (Barry, 2009: 254–25). In their analysis, ecocritics "emphasise ecocentric values of meticulous observation, collective ethical responsibility, and the claims of the world beyond ourselves" (Barry, 2009: 254–255).

Moroye (2007) took these ideas into education by experimenting with eco-educational criticism, which she describes in this way:

> Eco-educational criticism describes the particular ecological lens through which I filtered my observations and interpretations. By "ecological" I mean situations, ideas, and issues that address the inescapable embeddedness between and among humans and the natural environment including issues of care (Noddings, 2005), decision-making (Heimlich, 2002), sustainability, and global equity (Smith & Williams, 1999).
>
> *(p. 42)*

While this description of eco-educational criticism is not definitive, it allowed Moroye to filter her observations of "traditional" classrooms from an ecological lens for the purpose of understanding the significant practices operationalized by ecologically minded teachers. Such practices would likely go unnoticed if the ecological lens was absent.

Placing some of these above ideas along with a few others into the field of education, we would suggest the following:

1. Ecocritics pay attention to the kinds and orientations of texts used in schools and classrooms with an eye toward representations of the non-human world.
2. They extend the ecological vocabulary we might use to examine schools and classrooms.
3. They pay attention to the intentional, operational, and received curricula noting the congruence or lack thereof, with an eye toward the ecological significance of each for education generally speaking.

(New) aesthetic criticism

In her book *The Radical Aesthetic*, Isobel Armstrong (2000) creates a call to return to an examination of aesthetic ideas and principles found in literature. Reacting to the current anti-aesthetic trend, she says it this way:

> This book is about the turn to an anti-aesthetic in theoretical writing … The most influential cultural and literary theorists of the last two decades, even when they come from constituencies and traditions inimical to each other, have agreed – and sometimes it is all that they have agreed on – that the category of the aesthetic … is up for deconstruction.
>
> *(p. 1)*

Seen as a conservative and outmoded form of literary criticism, aesthetic critiques focus uniquely on each text. Armed with theories from various traditions including pragmatism, phenomenology, and cultural poetics, Armstrong brings fresh insights to understand the aesthetic aspects of literature. According to Barry (2009):

> It [new aestheticism] emphasizes the 'specificity' and 'particularity' of the literary text, seeking dialogue with it rather than mastery over it, and seeing the text as part of an on-going debate, within itself and with its readers, rather than viewing it as representative of a fixed position.
>
> *(p. 299)*

The focus on close reading is reminiscent of new criticism, but as just mentioned the goal is an opening-up of literature and not a closing-down. State Joughin and Malpas (2003):

> the recent resistance to aesthetics remains puzzling, not least insofar as many of the theoretical advances of the last years – the focus on the reader's role in the constitution of meaning, the possibility that texts are open to a number of interpretations, the way in which literature troubles fixed definitions of class, race, gender and sexuality, etc. – might themselves be brought together under the general rubric of 'the aesthetic function of literature.'
>
> *(p. 2)*

There is then a current literary movement that seeks to focus on the aesthetic features of the text as a place to unravel what the text does and what meaning might be made. We believe this kind of criticism makes sense given our Deweyan orientation in the first place (see Dewey, 1934). As we observe and try to understand any given object of focus, from poems to football to classrooms, one would do well to examine the particular features of specific contexts. What might we learn from this poem, this football game, or this specific classroom? Each has something to offer, and each most likely has something to teach – positively or negatively – the larger genre under which it fits (poems, football games, and classrooms). Since Eisner himself was greatly influenced by Dewey, one might wonder what differs between Eisner's conception of educational criticism and what we might call aesthetic educational criticism. The answer, in short, is that this approach pays particular attention to the aesthetic features of schools and classrooms. Summarizing this approach with its implications for education, one might note:

1. Aesthetic educational critics pay close attention to the aesthetic qualities of the contexts that they are studying: e.g., the quality and types of materials and their physical arrangements in the class. Also, they might note colors, sounds, textures, and even smells.
2. They also pay attention to "situated" factors that add meaning and understanding to the context under study.
3. They extend the aesthetic vocabulary we might use to examine schools and classrooms. For example, one may attend to the aesthetic category (Uhrmacher, 1991) to Eisner's ecology of schooling.
4. They pay attention to the intentional, operational, and received curricula noting the congruence or lack thereof, with an eye toward the aesthetic significance of each for education generally speaking. (See Kramer (2010) for an example of a study conducted using the aesthetic lens.)

Pragmatic race criticism

In our view, Cornel West (1989) revitalized American pragmatism with his book, *The American Evasion of Philosophy*. Pointing out the attractiveness of pragmatism, West writes, "For its major themes of evading epistemology-centered philosophy, accenting human powers, and transforming antiquated modes of social hierarchies in light of religious and/or ethical ideals make it relevant" (p. 4). He continues:

> American pragmatism is a diverse and heterogeneous tradition. But its common denominator consists of a future-oriented instrumentalism that tries to deploy thought as a weapon to enable more effective action. Its basic impulse is a plebian radicalism that fuels an antipatrician rebelliousness for the moral aim of enriching individuals and expanding democracy.
>
> *(p. 5)*

West traces pragmatism from Emerson, James, and Peirce to Richard Rorty and Roberto Unger, placing John Dewey at the epicenter. In his doing so, West pronounces what philosophy is before and after Dewey, "John Dewey is the culmination of the tradition of American pragmatism. After him, to be a pragmatist is to be a social critic, literary critic, or a poet – in short, a participant in cultural criticism and cultural creation" (p. 71). Not everyone may agree with West on this point about criticism, but we embrace it, as have some major writers such as Eddie Glaude Jr. Says Princeton professor Glaude, "I believe that the tradition of American pragmatism exemplified by Dewey offers powerful resources for redefining African American leadership and politics" (2007: x). Glaude seeks reflection and action among new leaders, and his book, *In a Shade of Blue: Pragmatism and the Politics of Black America*, contains six essays to point to new and imaginative possibilities.

In our view, a pragmatist approach to thinking about race provides opportunities not often found in other analytical tools such as critical race theory (CRT). To begin, a pragmatic approach is suspicious of essentializing racial categories, which while not necessarily a goal of CRT, is often the result. Second, a pragmatist approach situates race along with other complex factors. Dewey put it this way:

> The basis of race prejudice is instinctive dislike and dread of what is strange. This prejudice is converted into discrimination and friction by accidental physical features, and by cultural differences of language and religion, and especially at the present time, by an intermixture of political and economic forces. The result is the present concept of race of fixed racial differences and race friction. Scientifically, the concept of race is largely a fiction.
>
> *(Eldridge, in Lawson and Koch, 2004: 15)*

Dewey recognized that race is fictional but also that it is a necessary concept – at least temporarily – to resolve imperative problems. Echoing Dewey, Cornel West states:

> pragmatism … is a philosophical orientation that highlights history, context, and problem solving. You can't talk about race unless you talk about history; you can't talk about race unless you talk about changing context and history; and you can't talk about race unless you are really trying to wrestle with it and, I believe, trying to ameliorate the conditions that white supremacy produces … Now of course one needs social analytical tools. You really need an analysis of capitalist economy; you need an analysis of the relation of the economy to the state; you need an analysis of the relation of state to the educational system and its relationship to civil society in general. But as a philosophical orientation, pragmatism is ideal.
>
> *(in Lawson and Koch, 2004: 225)*

With the above in mind, CRT would be one tool among others that may be utilized to uncover and examine racial issues.

Finally, pragmatic race theorists would use the tools of reflection, discussion, and action as part of their arsenal. The goal is to test an idea in the real world and to examine its consequences. Pragmatism is not an armchair philosophical method. Pragmatism, says Cornel West, is about "experimentation" and "improvisation" that can be found in Ralph Waldo Emerson as well as Louis Armstrong. Says West, "And therefore to talk about America is to talk about improvisation and experimentation, and therefore to talk about Emerson and Louis Armstrong in the same breath" (1999: 543). Thus, action may take many forms. Summarizing:

1.   Race-focused educational critics pay close attention to the qualities of the contexts that they are studying with an eye toward matters of race.
2.   They also pay attention to "situated" factors that add meaning and understanding to the racial context under study.
3.   They extend the vocabulary we might use to examine schools and classrooms with the charge of understanding a new global America.
4.   They pay attention to the intentional, operational, and received curricula noting the congruence or lack thereof, with an eye toward the significance of each for diverse students.

Newer strategies

We presented three theories that we believe are useful for educational critics. Each of these, along with the 12 others mentioned, may be utilized as interpretive frameworks that guide and provide meaning to one's study. Now, to conclude this chapter, we would also like to lay out what we see as new opportunities.

Mixed methods and forms of representation

Related to conjoining educational criticism with other types of qualitative research, as we mentioned earlier, is the idea of using educational criticism in a mixed methods approach. Patterson's (1997) dissertation is an example of using survey data along with educational criticism. In addition, as we also discussed above, educational criticism may utilize various forms of representation. Elliot Eisner had emphatically and cogently argued for researchers to utilize various forms of representation, and by this he meant that one learns through pictures and audio, theatre and dance, rap poems, and sonnets. As human beings we choose to express ourselves through a variety of means and not just the written word alone. Thus, we would suggest that researchers may substitute linguistic descriptions such as prose and poetry with other forms of representation – an installation art exhibit, a play, a dance performance, a musical score, etc. Staying true to what we see as the role of the critic, however, we would argue that these forms still need elaboration. That is, the critic would need to interpret the dance, the musical score, as well as evaluate and thematicize what may be learned. There are researchers who believe that something like an installation art exhibit should be able to stand on its own, and that written words explaining the exhibit are not needed and may even be considered distracting. Perhaps this is the case, but at least at this point in time we would suggest that those following the method of educational criticism still consider utilizing interpretations, evaluations, and thematics along with the description. In our view, the critic, unlike the artist, has the task of explanation.

Auto-criticism

Another line of inquiry might be called auto-criticism. In the same way that some educational researchers have used autobiography, while others in education with an interest in cultural matters have employed auto-ethnography, we would also suggest that researchers consider the appellation of auto-criticism. Whereas autobiography often tells a story without analytic categories to assist the researcher in unpacking one's life, narrative and auto-ethnography stem from an anthropological tradition that focuses on culture. Auto-criticism would differ from each; it would employ analytic categories and would still require interpretation and evaluation. It would not, however, be bound to culture; rather, it could include analytic categories that stem from aesthetics and ecology, as well as some combination of race, class, gender, and/or religion. Thus, one may write about one's own life in the contexts of being a teacher, a principal, a social worker, a nurse, or a business leader, and in doing so, one would want to interpret one's own narrative with categories that bring new intellectual ideas to life. What is it like, for example, to be a Latina medic in a mostly male profession? Or, what is it like to be a teacher dedicated to global warming in a community insensitive or even hostile to this idea?

Criticism and action research

Another combination one might explore is educational criticism with action research in general and participatory action research (PAR) in particular. Generally speaking, while there are variations on the method, action research often involves problem-finding, hypotheses, actions, and reflections. Then, depending on the results of the first cycle, the process repeats. The goal is to improve one's actual practice. What criticism has to offer is in the problem-finding and reflective aspects of the cycle. We suggest that action researchers place their problem-finding in descriptive, interpretive, and evaluative formats. That is, first, action researchers would want to describe the context they intend to investigate. Second, they would want to interpret the problematic situation and ask what the various reasons for the problem are? Next, after settling on a particular reason for the problem and devising an action strategy to remedy it, an action research approach with educational criticism elements would also want to use description, interpretation, and evaluation as a way to reflect on whether the actions worked. In this approach one would redescribe what happened, reinterpret the findings, and evaluate what needs to be done subsequently.

Before moving on, a word about participatory action research and educational criticism. According to Pant (2014):

> PAR combines research and action through a cyclic or spiral process which alternates between action and critical reflection. It lays emphasis on authenticity rather than on the scientific validity of the information. Therefore, statistically significant and generalizable conclusions are generally avoided.
>
> *(p. 585)*

By utilizing educational criticism, one takes the research out of the scientific perspective in the first place. Second when combining these two approaches, we would suggest that action researchers from the university who are working with a local population consider writing educational critiques that would be useful in the reflective stage of the research. For example, researchers might write educational criticisms for the community to read and these would provide the basis for reflection.

A return to evaluation

In his seminal article titled "Elliot Eisner's Lost Legacy," Robert Donmoyer (2014) reminds readers that Eisner began "his signature work on arts-based research by writing about program evaluation" (p. 442). As such, this section is not so much about creating a new line of thinking about research, but rather returning to a set of ideas that have been cast out years ago. Donmoyer discusses arts-based research, which allows for a variety of forms of representation and therefore his essay is about more than educational criticism. But we would stress, and we think Donmoyer would agree, that educational criticism as a method with roots in the arts is particularly suited to these ideas on program evaluation. First, educational criticism as evaluation places special emphasis on perception. Donmoyer notes that Eisner did not have much to say about procedures and in part that is because Eisner wanted evaluations to focus on being in the context of the evaluation and really "seeing" what was taking place. Donmoyer states: "the contribution of evaluation is in the area of problem framing; evaluators provide decision makers with new ways to conceptualize issues" (p. 449). Second, Donmoyer points out that evaluators ought to consider various ways of displaying their data. As we indicated with participatory action research, educational criticism is a form of representation that has the opportunity to bring the recipient (either a reader of the text or a listener to a reading of the text) into cognitive as well as emotional spaces to create an impact. Third, Donmoyer points to a focus on imagination as another major contribution that Eisner made to the field of evaluation. We quote Donmoyer at some length to make this point:

> evaluation work inevitably has an imaginative component. Some evaluators may want to embrace this dimension of evaluation work wholeheartedly – as connoisseurs (who see and make meaning of the nuances in the programs they study and then artfully disclose their critiques) do. Others, undoubtedly, will be content to frame their empirical investigations around what the developers of the programs they are evaluating have imagined, as is the case when evaluators use program developers' logic models to frame and direct their empirical work. Even when professional evaluators take the latter pathway, however, someone's imaginings are providing a foundation for an evaluation's empirical investigations. Whatever imaginings evaluators use and wherever they come from, the imaginative elements of an evaluation study have the potential to creep into some decision makers' heads and influence some decision-making process somewhere, normally in unpredictable but potentially significant ways.
>
> *(p. 442)*

We end then by noting that educational critics – as well as critics of other types of environments – ought to revisit Eisner's ideas in respect to evaluation. We would also suggest that one begin one's journey in this arena by taking a look at Donmoyer's essay.

Exploring new forms of the essay

Finally, we would like to suggest that educational critics continue to use and explore the form of the essay as a way to convey their ideas. About the essay, Donald Hall (1995) had this to say:

> Often one literary form dominates an era. In Shakespeare's time the play was the thing, and lyric poets ... wrote for the stage when they turned aside from their primary work. A few decades ago, American novelists wrote novels when they could afford to but paid their bills by writing short stories for Collier's and the Saturday Evening Post. Today novelists of similar eminence and ability ... become performers of the essay, for we live in the age of the essay.
>
> *(p. 1)*

While noting that the third edition of the book *The Contemporary Essay* came out in 1995, we hold that Hall's observation is still true today. Why? Hall provides a clear answer: "Our age needs the essay because it requires exposition. We live in a time bewildered by the multiplicity of information; we cherish the selection and organization of information by our best writers" (p. 1).

While there are notable exceptions (see Barone, 1983), utilized mostly in dissertations, many educational criticisms have taken the form of data presentation with lengthy literary descriptions. And since data presentation is often in a chapter four while conclusions are in Chapter 5, the critic does not write in an essay format.

While one must be careful in writing for specific audiences, we would suggest that critics consider the contemporary essay as a literary format for presentation. In doing so, the new form of the educational criticism will allow new possibilities. First and foremost, the essay provides an opportunity to create connections across three different registers (or types of writing). The writer Aldous Huxley (1958) sees it this way:

> Essays belong to a literary species whose extreme variability can be studied most effectively within a three-poled frame of reference. There is the pole of the personal and the autobiographical; there is the pole of the objective, the factual, the concrete-particular; and there is the pole of the abstract–universal.
>
> *(p. v)*

The most richly satisfying essays are those which make the best not of one, not of two, but of all the three worlds in which it is possible for the essay to exist.

(p. vii)

While most types of academic writing push researchers to stay within one of the poles that Huxley mentions, the essay allows the researcher to cross boundaries and make connections among the personal, the factual, and the cosmic all in one piece.

Essayist Mikhail Epstein (1995) puts it this way:

> An essay may be philosophical, artistic, critical, historical, autobiographical, but the essential fact remains that as a rule it is everything at once. These attributes may interconnect variously in any one instance, one will predominate, while another steps aside, but in principle, all existing realms of consciousness are able to become components of an essayistic work.
>
> *(p. 213)*

The essay allows what Deleuze might call rhizomatic possibilities (Colebrook, 2002). That is, the essay allows cuts across genres of research, writing, and experience, and places them together in a way that each enriches and enlightens the other. The upshot of this is a heightened, dare we say, aesthetic experience for the reader. Surely this kind of knowing opens up doors of perception. Subsequently, one may see school and classrooms – or whatever the object of focus may be – in new lights.

Conclusion

For those of you still reading along, you may note that we have taken you through a journey that explores the past, present, and future of educational criticism. We have tried to provide you with tools and advice on how to do this kind of research in a practical sense; we have also given you some of the conceptual underpinnings of educational criticism and connoisseurship so that you may defend it, if you must, from those unfamiliar with this kind of methodology. Not that long ago, Locke and Riley asked, what happened to educational criticism in their 2009 essay of the same title. We are pleased to say that educational criticism is alive and well. If you haven't already, come join us in the adventure of writing criticisms. In doing so, you will open up new doors of perception for yourself and others, with perhaps attendant actions to make our worlds a better place to live, work, and play.

Reflective questions and activities

1. Take a picture of a setting such as your desk, a park, or a coffee shop. Then, before you look at the picture, describe the setting you are observing with words. Now, compare your description with the picture. What do you notice? What does the picture reveal that the written description does not? What do the words help you see that is not attained through the picture?

2. Are you working somewhere that other people find intriguing? Can you imagine writing about 75 pages on yourself? Write down heading and sub-headings of your experience that you would want to explore and express to others.

3. Some of the ideas and procedures used in educational criticism may be used in conjunction with other research methods such as grounded theory, phenomenology, and ethnography. Take one method that interests you (let's say portraiture) and write down how the two methods might assist each other in terms of observation, interviewing, data analysis, or writing.

Educational criticism is not a fixed method, and its features may be altered to use non-linguistic forms of representation. Educational criticism may be used to examine non-educational settings. If you are interested in studying yourself as a subject of a particular context, consider writing an auto-criticism.

Note

1 Carolyn Mears eventually created her own research method which she calls the gateway approach (2009).

References

Armstrong, I. (2000). *The radical aesthetic*. Oxford, UK: Blackwell.

Barone, T. (1983). Things of use and things of beauty: The Swain County high school arts program. *Daedalus, 1*, 1–28.

Barry, P. (2009). *Beginning theory: An introduction to literary and cultural theory*. Manchester, UK: Manchester University Press.

Beck, H. (2003). Nontraditional superintendents: Perceptions of their performance and current hiring trends (unpublished doctoral dissertation). University of Denver, Denver, CO.

Best, S. and Kellner, D. (1991). Postmodern theory: Critical interrogations. New York: Guilford Press.

Bressler, C. E. (1999). *Literary criticism: An introduction to theory and practice*. Upper Saddle River, NJ: Prentice Hall.

Bunn, K. (2009). Bridging policy and education (unpublished doctoral dissertation). University of Denver, Denver, CO.

Cloninger, K. (2008). Transcending curriculum ideologies: Educating human beings well. (unpublished doctoral dissertation). University of Denver, Denver, CO.

Colebrook, C. (2002). *Gilles Deleuze*. New York: Routledge.

Denison, C. W. (1994). The children of EST: A study of the experience and perceived effects of a large group awareness training (The Forum) (unpublished doctoral dissertation). University of Denver, Denver, CO.

Dewey, J. (1934). *Art as experience*. New York: Perigee Books.

Donmoyer, R. (2014). Elliot Eisner's lost legacy. *American Journal of Evaluation, 35*(3), 442–452.

Eagleton, T. (1983). *Literary theory*. Minneapolis, MN: Minneapolis University Press.

Eisner, E. W. (1982). Toward an artistic approach to supervision. *Yearbook of the Association for Supervision and Curriculum Development*. Washington, DC.

Eisner, E. W. (1988). The ecology of school improvement. *Educational Leadership*, 45(5), 24–24.

Eisner, E. W. (1991). *The enlightened eye: Qualitative inquiry and the enhancement of educational practice*. New York: Macmillan.

Eisner, E. W. and Peshkin, A. (Eds.). (1990). *Qualitative inquiry in education: The continuing debate*. New York: Teachers College Press.

Ellison, R. ([1952] 1995). *Invisible man*. New York: Vintage.

Epstein, M. (1995). *After the future: The paradoxes of postmodernism and contemporary Russian culture* (trans. Anesa Miller-Pogacar). Amherst, MA: University of Massachusetts Press.

Garrard, G. (2012). *Ecocriticism* (2nd ed.). New York: Routledge.

Getz, L. B. (1997). The effects of Colorado State Educational Standards on independent school curricula (unpublished doctoral dissertation). University of Denver, Denver, CO.

Glaude, E. S. (2007). *In a shade of blue: Pragmatism and the politics of black America*. Chicago, IL: University of Chicago Press.

Hall, D. (1995) (3rd ed.). *The contemporary essay*. Boston, MA: Bedford Books of St. Martin's Press.

Huxley, A. (1958). *Collected essays*. New York: Harper & Row.

Joughin, J. J. and Malpas, S. (2003). *The new aestheticism*. Manchester, UK: Manchester University Press.

Kramer, J. (2010). Closer to the heart: An exploration of caring and creative visual arts classrooms (unpublished doctoral dissertation). University of Denver, Denver, CO.

Lawson, B. E. and Koch, D. (Eds.). (2004). *Pragmatism and the problem of race*. Bloomington, IN: University of Indiana Press.

Lincoln, Y. S. (1995). Emerging criteria for quality in qualitative and interpretive research. *Qualitative inquiry*, 1(3), 275–289.

Locke, T. and Riley, D. (2009). What happened to educational criticism? Engaging with a paradigm for observation. *Educational Action Research*, 17(4), 489–504.

Mears, C. (2005). Experiences of Columbine parents: Finding a way to tomorrow (unpublished doctoral dissertation). University of Denver, Denver, CO.

Mears, C. L. (2009). *Interviewing for education and social science research: The gateway approach*. London, UK: Palgrave Macmillan.

Moroye, C. M. (2007). Greening our future: The practices of ecologically minded teachers. Retrieved from ProQuest Digital Dissertations (3253733).

Morrell, E. (2004). *Becoming critical researchers: Literacy and empowerment for urban youth*. New York: Peter Lang.

Orr, D. (1992). *Ecological literacy: Education and the transition to a postmodern world*. Albany, NY: State University of New York Press.

Pant, M. (2014). Participatory action research. In D. Coghlan, and M. Brydon-Miller (Eds.), *The SAGE encyclopedia of action research* (pp. 584–589). Thousand Oaks, CA: Sage.

Patterson, R. J. (1997). Qualitative inquiry into artists in residence of Colorado (unpublished doctoral dissertation). University of Denver, Denver, CO.

Pope, Alexander (1711). An essay on criticism. Retrieved from www.poetryfoundation.org/learning/essay/237826 (last accessed: February 15, 2016).

Uhrmacher, P. B. (1991). Waldorf schools marching quietly unheard (unpublished doctoral dissertation). Stanford, CA, Stanford University.

Uhrmacher, P. B. and Matthews, J. (Eds.). (2005). *Intricate palette: Working the ideas of Elliot Eisner*. Columbus, OH: Merrill Prentice Hall.

Vanderbrook, C. (2005). Gifted girls in AP and IB programs (unpublished doctoral dissertation). University of Denver, Denver, CO.

Welleck, R. (1981). Literary criticism. In P. Hernadi (Ed.), *What is criticism?* Bloomington, ID: Indiana University Press.

West, C. (1989). *The American evasion of philosophy: A genealogy of pragmatism.* Madison, WI: University of Wisconsin Press.

West, C. (1999). *The Cornel West reader.* New York: Civitas Books.

Yalom, I. D. (1985). *The theory and practice of group psychotherapy* (3rd ed.). New York: Basis Books.

INDEX

Made in the USA
Columbia, SC
04 January 2024

29873626R10057